Grade 3

Carson-Dellosa Publishing LLC
Greensboro, North Carolina

Credits
Content Editor: Christine Schwab
Copy Editor: Angela Triplett

Visit *carsondellosa.com* for correlations to Common Core, state, national, and Canadian provincial standards.

Carson-Dellosa Publishing LLC
PO Box 35665
Greensboro, NC 27425 USA
carsondellosa.com

ISBN 978-1-4838-4168-7
02-190181151

Table of Contents

Introduction

Language Arts 4 Today: Daily Skill Practice is a comprehensive yet quick and easy-to-use supplement to any classroom language arts curriculum. This series will strengthen students' reading skills as they review comprehension, fluency, vocabulary, and decoding skills. Students' writing skills will improve as they practice parts of speech, grammar, and spelling.

This book covers 40 weeks of daily practice. Essential language arts skills are reviewed each day during a four-day period with an assessment of the skills practiced on the fifth day. Each week includes a fluency practice section, intended to be a quick one-minute activity that encourages fluency in reading and recognition of sight words. For more detailed fluency tips, see pages 5 and 6. The week concludes with a writing journal prompt.

Various skills and concepts are reinforced throughout the book through activities that align to the state standards. To view these standards, see the Standards Alignment Chart on page 7.

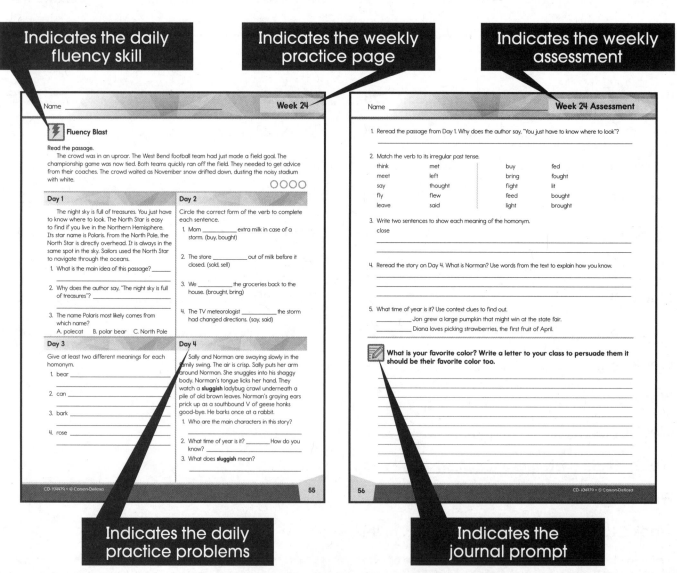

Indicates the daily fluency skill

Indicates the weekly practice page

Indicates the weekly assessment

Indicates the daily practice problems

Indicates the journal prompt

Developing Fluency

Fluency is the ability to read accurately, effortlessly, and with proper expression while comprehending the text. A growing number of studies have identified reading fluency as an important factor in student reading success.

The Four Components of Fluency

- *Accuracy* involves reading words correctly. Accuracy matters the most when the reader's mistakes change the meaning of the text.
- *Rate* is the ability to move through the text at the proper pace. Moving too fast or too slow through the text should not interfere with the reader's expression, voice, or comprehension.
- *Expression* is a reader's voice expression. Expression can indicate comprehension as the reader adjusts his voice to show the tone or mood of the text.
- *Phrasing* indicates the reader can move smoothly through the text in meaningful phrases with careful regard to punctuation.

Using the Fluency Blast

Students should read the weekly fluency blast passage (or sight words) for the week every day (excluding assessment day). They will then color one bubble for each reading. Use one or a combination of the following ways to read the passages (or sight words):

- Set a timer for one minute (or 30 seconds for faster readers). Have students read the passage and mark the last word read. Students should try to improve on the number of words read per minute each day.
- Allow students to read at their own pace each day.
- Students can read the passage while focusing on a particular word work skill, such as marking the prefixes or suffixes in the passage.
- Have students read the passage in silly voices. You can even assign a voice for the day, such as reading the passage like a monster, older person, pirate, etc.
- Students can buddy read the passage, taking turns being the "reader" and the "listener," and then offering feedback to their partners.
- Read the passage as a choral reading with the entire class.

Tracking Fluency

Have students use the reproducible on page 6 to track their progress and develop goals for improving their fluency. This page can be used quarterly, weekly, or biweekly. Have students request feedback from their peers when the reproducible is used with buddy reading.

Name _____

Date _____

Reading Fluency Evaluation

	What I think			What my peer thinks		
Accuracy Did I read the words correctly?	:)	:|	:(	:)	:|	:(
Rate Was my reading just right, not too slow and not too fast?	:)	:|	:(	:)	:|	:(
Expression Did I read with feeling so that I did not sound like a robot?	:)	:|	:(	:)	:|	:(
Phrasing Did I pay attention to the punctuation marks as I read?	:)	:|	:(	:)	:|	:(

A Goal I Will Try to Meet Next Time

_____ I will read more slowly.

_____ I will read faster.

_____ I will use more expression.

_____ I will consider the punctuation.

Standards Alignment Chart

State Standards*		Weeks
Reading Standards for Literature		
Key Ideas and Details	3.RL.1–3.RL.3	1–40
Craft and Structure	3.RL.4–3.RL.6	1–4, 6, 16, 17, 19, 21–24, 26, 30, 32, 33, 38–40
Integration of Knowledge and Ideas	3.RL.7, 3.RL.9	1–3, 5, 8, 10, 11, 13, 15, 18, 20–22, 24, 25, 27, 28, 30, 31, 34
Range of Reading and Level of Text Complexity	3.RL.10	1–40
Reading Standards for Informational Text		
Key Ideas and Details	3.RI.1–3.RI.3	1–40
Craft and Structure	3.RI.4–3.RI.6	1–3, 5–8, 10, 11, 12, 14, 15, 17, 18, 20, 22, 24–28, 30, 33–39
Integration of Knowledge and Ideas	3.RI.7–3.RI.9	1, 3, 5–7, 9, 14, 16, 17, 23, 25–30, 40
Range of Reading and Level of Text Complexity	3.RI.10	1–40
Writing Standards		
Each week includes a journal writing prompt to cover writing standards.		
Reading Standards: Foundational Skills		
Phonics, Word Recognition, and Fluency	3.RF.3–3.RF.4	1–40
Language Standards		
Conventions of Standard English	3.L.1–3.L.2	1–40
Knowledge of Language	3.L.3	3, 4, 14, 17, 24, 26, 27, 34, 35, 38
Vocabulary Acquisition and Use	3.L.4–3.L.6	1–40

School-to-Home Connection

The research is clear that family involvement is strongly linked to student success. Support for student learning at home improves student achievement in school. Educators should not underestimate the significance of this connection.

The fluency activities in this book create an opportunity to create or improve this school-to-home link. Students are encouraged to read their fluency passage or sight words at home with their families each week. Parents and guardians can use the reproducible tracking sheet (below) to record how their student performed in their fluency activities during the week. Students should be encouraged to return their tracking sheets to the teacher at the end of the week.

In order to make the school-to-home program work for students and their families, it may be helpful to reach out to them with an introductory letter. Explain the program and its intent and ask them to partner with you in their children's educational process. Describe the role you expect them to play. Encourage them to offer suggestions or feedback along the way.

 Fluency at Home   Name _____

- **Get Ready**—Get the passage (or sight words) for the week. Set a timer for one minute.

- **Get Set**—Start the timer when your student starts reading.

- **Go!** Mark any misread words. Record the total number of words your student read.

Week Number	1st reading words per minute	2nd reading words per minute	3rd reading words per minute	4th reading words per minute
	_____ /wpm	_____ /wpm	_____ /wpm	_____ /wpm
Problem words or phrases				

Fluency Blast

Read the passage.

Snow is a lot of fun. It is wet and cold, but you can do so many things with it. You can make snowballs and throw them at a target. You can make forts, igloos, and snowmen from snow. You need it for sledding down a hill, and no one could make snow angels without it. Snow is a lot of fun.

○○○○

Day 1

The Navajo tribes lived in the southwestern United States. Their homes, called **hogans**, were made of wood and mud. A hogan's door always faced east. This way, the morning sun shone inside the house. The Navajo people believed that the sun brought ideas and planning.

1. Underline the text that tells the main idea of this passage.

2. What is a **hogan**? _____

3. Why was it important that the hogan door faced east? _____
_____
_____

4. Write the compound word from the text.
_____

Day 2

I would love to be in charge of the world. I would make a rule that everybody could have their own rooms, even twins. I would lock my door so that no one could mess with my stuff!

1. Name one proper noun used in the passage.
_____

2. What would an adult say instead of "mess with my stuff?"
_____
_____

3. What rule would you make if you were in charge of the world?
_____
_____

Day 3

Sometimes I want to answer a question so badly, my body seems to lift into the air by itself. It's like I am controlled by aliens. Before I know it, I am standing at my seat. If I'm not careful, I might also jump in the air or wave wildly. I know teachers dislike when students do this. So, I quickly sit down and restrain myself.

1. Underline each prefix in the passage.

2. Circle each suffix in the passage.

3. Write how many syllables are in each word.

_____ question   _____ aliens

_____ teachers   _____ students

Day 4

I live on the third floor of an apartment building. My family has lived there for nine years. It is a beautiful building. It has a playground out back. It is the best part about living there. The playground has swings, a slide, and monkey bars. I can play with other kids from my apartment building.

1. Do you think the building is in a town or city? _____ How can you tell?
_____

2. Compare the home in this passage with the home described on Day 1. How are they different? Alike? _____
_____
_____

1. Circle the compound words. Underline each part.

   toothpick   lipstick   soccer   bookmark   runaway

2. Write three proper nouns. Use correct capitalization.

   _____   _____   _____

3. List the prefix and suffix for each word.

   unforgettable   _____   _____

   preschooler   _____   _____

   distasteful   _____   _____

   rereading   _____   _____

4. Compare the themes of the stories in Day 1 and Day 4. How are they alike? _____

   How are they different? _____

   _____

5. Look back to the story on Day 4. Write the opposite of each word.

   ugly   _____   front   _____   here   _____

   work   _____   your   _____   worst   _____

✏️ **Write about your home. Tell what it looks like inside and out. What makes it different from other homes you have visited?**

_____

_____

_____

_____

_____

_____

_____

_____

_____

_____

_____

Fluency Blast

Read the passage.

Salt and Pepper were born in the same month. They lived together at Bill's Pet Palace. Salt was a white kitten. Her crate sat in the front window beside a black puppy. He was named Pepper. The two animals had become best friends. Bill hoped he could find a family who would take them both.

○○○○

Day 1

Japan has a holiday just for girls and a holiday just for boys. But, Japan has holidays for the whole family too. April is the month for the Cherry Blossom Festival. It is a **festival** for the whole family. In April, everyone goes to see the cherry trees. They bloom for one week.

1. What does the word **festival** mean? _____
   _____

2. What country is this passage about?
   _____

3. When is the Cherry Blossom Festival?
   _____

4. Will people celebrate the Cherry Blossom Festival inside or outside? _____

Day 2

1. Replace each name with the correct pronoun.
   (John) _____ took (Ruby's) _____ pencil and broke it.
   (The kids) _____ heard (the band) _____ play music.

2. Choose the correct verb to complete each sentence.
   Because he was late, Derek (bring, brought) a note from home.
   I will have to (think, thought) about it for a while.
   Angela (speak, spoke) in a quiet voice.
   It wasn't what I (mean, meant) to say.

Day 3

Dez is in a hurry. She forgot to set her alarm last night. So, it did not wake her in time. Now, she is late for school. She runs down the hallway and crashes into Gerard, who is carrying his science project. He had done an **environmental** study of the creek area behind his house. His samples go flying!

1. What does the word **environmental** mean?
   _____

2. Why was Dez late for school? _____
   _____

3. What do you think an **environmental** study is?
   _____
   _____

Day 4

Pitter and Patter are two drops of water. They are great friends who usually travel the water cycle together. One day, they were separated in the middle of a puddle. Later, Pitter and Patter met up again in a cloud. After a joyful **reunion**, the two told their stories.

1. Underline the words in the text that tell who or what the main characters are.

2. What does **reunion** mean? _____
   _____

3. How does this fictional story relate to the real water cycle?
   _____
   _____

---

1. What other facts would you like to learn about Japan? _____
_____

   Why? _____

2. Choose the correct pronoun to complete the sentences.

   The skateboarder flew off of (him, his) board.

   I handed each of (their, them) five ride tickets.

   The cat purred in (her, its) arms.

   Give me (my, their) book back!

3. Match each verb to the irregular verb.

   catch   bit

   bite   stuck

   leave   flew

   throw   left

   stick   threw

   fly   caught

4. Use the word **environment** in a sentence.

   _____
   _____

✏️ **Tell about a holiday your family celebrates. How do they celebrate?**

_____
_____
_____
_____
_____
_____
_____
_____
_____
_____

Fluency Blast

Read the passage.

One day, as Kit walked to school, she noticed a purple dog flying over the treetops near her house. The dog looked familiar. "Why, that's my dog!" she exclaimed. "That's my dog, Bailey. Why is his fur purple? He's a golden retriever!" She tried to think, then sputtered, "And why is he flying so high? He knows he shouldn't do that!"

○ ○ ○ ○

Day 1

An eclipse of the sun is called a solar eclipse. **Solar** means sun. A solar eclipse happens when the sun's light is blocked from Earth. This happens when the moon passes exactly between the sun and Earth. The sun's light is blocked by the moon. During a total eclipse, Earth becomes dark. A solar eclipse is an amazing event.

1. What does **solar** mean? _____

2. How does an eclipse happen? _____
   _____
   _____

3. How does the author feel about solar eclipses?
   _____
   _____

Day 2

1. Rewrite this passage using correct capitalization and punctuation.

   jacques cousteau explored many of earths oceans he believed it was important to protect ocean life. He created a group called the Cousteau Society more than 50,000 people belong to it today

   _____
   _____
   _____
   _____
   _____
   _____

Day 3

Arrange the syllables to form a familiar word.

1. tas fan tic _____

2. mem re ber _____

3. le te phone _____

4. ger bur ham _____

5. ta mins vi _____

Day 4

Jason picked another quarter from the vine and put it in his basket. It clinked merrily as it joined the pile of big silver coins. This was the second week in a row that his plants were providing him with coins. He looked down the long row of money plants. He smiled. His money plants were going to make him rich.

1. From whose point of view is this story told?
   _____

2. Do you think this passage is fiction or nonfiction? Explain. _____
   _____

3. What would you do if you found a money plant? _____
   _____

1. Use the word **solar** in a sentence.

   _____

2. Reread the passage on Day 1. What was the author's purpose in writing about solar eclipses?

   _____

3. Circle the words that should be capitalized. Add the correct punctuation.

   do you know anything about the loch ness monster she is called nessie

4. Rewrite the words to divide them into syllables.

   elephant _____

   acrobat _____

   gravity _____

   ladybug _____

   multiply _____

5. Jason said that his money plants would make him rich. What could happen that might make this untrue?

   _____

   _____

   _____

Use descriptive language to write about a dream you remember. What do you think it meant?

_____

_____

_____

_____

_____

_____

_____

_____

_____

Fluency Blast

Read the passage.

If you place your tongue on ice-cold metal, it will stick. Your warm tongue melts the frozen surface of the metal. Then, the icy metal refreezes. It can stick to the wet surface of your tongue. Your tongue may stay frozen to the metal. Ouch! Do not try this at home or anywhere!

○○○○

Day 1

Unpleasant sounds are called **noise**. Some noises can be harmful to your hearing. Loud noises, such as those from airplanes or machines, can even cause a hearing loss. But other sounds, such as music or talking, are not dangerous. They are just pleasant.

1. What is this passage about? _____

2. What is **noise**? _____

3. Write the two antonyms found in the passage.

   _____

   _____

4. Write the two synonyms found in the passage.

   _____

   _____

Day 2

Circle the adverb and draw an arrow from the adverb to the word it describes.

1. I fell off of my bike yesterday.

2. Jamie caught the ball easily.

3. The dogs can play outside by themselves.

4. The water in the pot boiled over.

Day 3

The Channel 4 weather woman had a disagreement with the Channel 6 weather man. He said, "There may be a chance of freezing tonight." She said there is definitely a chance of freezing tonight. "In fact," she said, "I would overlook that nonsense if it wasn't already 25 degrees outside!"

1. Underline each prefix in the passage.

2. Circle each suffix in the passage.

3. Write how many syllables are in each word.

   _____ meteorologist _____ disagreement

   _____ definitely _____ nonsense

Day 4

Anita ran to the window. She thought she heard a helicopter until she saw how big it was. She called to Miguel. "Look," she whispered. "What do you think that is?" Miguel's eyes were **as big as dinner plates**. "I think an **alien** spaceship just landed in our yard!"

1. Who are the main characters in this story?

   _____

2. What does **alien** mean? _____

   _____

3. What does the author mean when she says Miguel's eyes were **as big as dinner plates**?

   _____

   _____

1. Write a synonym for each word.

   start _____   simple _____

   observe _____   unusual _____

2. Write an antonym for each word.

   subtract _____   forward _____

   shiny _____   loose _____

3. In each sentence, circle the adverb that describes the underlined verb.

   The prince slowly <u>climbed</u> Rapunzel's long hair.

   Little Red Riding Hood <u>returned</u> home yesterday.

   The wolf <u>hid</u> outside.

4. List the prefix and suffix for each word.

   unforgettable   _____   _____

   preschooler   _____   _____

   distasteful   _____   _____

   rereading   _____   _____

5. What does it mean when someone says that a person is "all ears"?

   _____

   _____

___

✏️ **Tell about a sound you do not like to hear. Explain why.**

_____

_____

_____

_____

_____

_____

_____

_____

_____

Fluency Blast

Read the passage.

When a wolf wants to play, she looks much like any other playful dog. The wolf will go down on her front paws with her tail in the air like she is bowing. Her tail will wag. It will appear as if the wolf is smiling with her tongue hanging out. Anyone can tell that she is behaving in a playful manner.

○ ○ ○ ○

Day 1

Many Inuit people live in the Canadian Arctic. How do they find food in the winter? They may go ice fishing. First, Inuit people put on warm clothes. Then, they find a lake that is covered with ice. The ice fishers walk out across the ice. The ice must be thick so that the ice fishers do not fall into the water.

1. Where do some Inuit people live? _____
   _____

2. Describe the setting of the passage. _____
   _____

3. What does the ice have to be like for safe ice fishing? _____
   _____
   _____

Day 2

1. Read the paragraph. Circle the words that should be capitalized. Add the correct punctuation.

   saturday, july 7, was lily's birthday lily and

   mom decided that a movie marathon would

   be fun lily picked her three favorite movies

   mom made popcorn grandpa henry made

   strawberry and chocolate ice-cream shakes

   lily could not wait for her friends gabe

   tamiko eliza and ben to arrive

Day 3

Circle the correctly spelled word from each set.

1. especially   especilly   aspecially

2. beatiful   beautifil   beautiful

3. impossable   impossible   inpossible

4. peeple   poeple   people

Day 4

Mario helped his father grill the burgers. First, Mario patted lumps of hamburger into patties. Next, he sprinkled salt and pepper on them. Fifteen minutes later, he turned them over. It wasn't long before his father told him they were ready to eat. Mario tasted his burger. It was a masterpiece!

1. What happened first? _____
   _____

   What happened next? _____
   _____

   What happened last? _____

2. What do you think Mario's father was doing during this time? _____
   _____

1. Reread the passage on Day 1. Why did the author write this text?

   _____

2. Rewrite each sentence with correct capitalization and punctuation.

   michelle wie's family is korean _____

   memorial day and labor day always fall on a monday _____

   _____

3. Write the dates correctly.

   saturday, july 4 _____

   thursday, september 18 _____

   friday, december 23 _____

4. Cross out each misspelled word and write the correct spelling above it.

   Turn rite after you pass the liberry, and then look for a wite house.

5. If you had one of Mario's hamburgers off the grill, how would you prepare it for eating? Write the steps in the correct order.

   _____

   _____

   _____

What is one food dish you know how to make yourself? Tell how you make it. Include the steps and ingredients.

   _____

   _____

   _____

   _____

   _____

   _____

   _____

   _____

   _____

   _____

Fluency Blast

Read the passage.

Bits was a small, gray squirrel. She lived in a big maple tree on Allan Road. She had a nice, dry nest in the big, old tree. Lots of trees grew nearby where she could always find nuts and seeds. There was a little stream she could drink from when she was thirsty. Bits had a happy life . . . until someone new moved into the neighborhood.

○○○○

Day 1

You might think a spider is an insect. But, it is not! These creatures belong to another animal family. They are arachnids. Arachnids have four pairs of legs and two body parts. Spiders make webs from strings of silk. They trap insects in their webs. The insects stick to the **gooey** silk. They become food for the spider.

1. Describe an arachnid's body. _____
   _____
   _____

2. How do spiders get their food? _____
   _____

3. What does **gooey** mean? _____
   _____

Day 2

I have a pen pal who lives in France, said Louie. I know a few words in French and he knows a few words in English. Sarah Kate said, My pen pal is from Australia. We both speak English. Then, she giggled. But, it doesn't sound the same when we speak!

1. Place quotation marks in the passage where they belong.

2. List the proper nouns in the passage.

   _____   _____

   _____   _____

   _____   _____

   _____

Day 3

Underline the vowel team in each set of words. Then, circle the word in each set that breaks the rule by not making the same vowel team sound.

1. each   stream   break   please

2. waist   said   brain   raise

3. brown   tower   gown   grown

4. crouch   mouth   rough   house

5. shawl   lawyer   yawn   straw

Day 4

In seven years, I will be 15! Then, I can become a **squire**. A squire does whatever his master wants. Later, he is trained to ride into battle with his master. Squires compete in a contest called **jousting**. One squire tries to knock the other squire off his horse with a long lance.

1. How old is the author? _____

2. How does he feel about becoming a squire?
   _____

3. What is a **squire**? _____
   _____

4. What is **jousting**? _____
   _____

1. Place quotation marks in the sentences where they belong.

   This summer, I'm going to take Spanish lessons, said McKenzie

   Our suitcases are in the attic, Dad said.

   Ryan said, I plan to swim at the lake every day.

2. Look around the room. Write four proper nouns.

   _____   _____   _____   _____

3. Complete each word with the correct vowel team (**-ea**, **-ai**, **-ow**, **-ou**, **-aw**).

   dr_____m   dr_____   s_____nd   pr_____rie   cr_____d

4. Read the passage. Circle the words with vowel teams. Read each one aloud.

   I had a dream the other night that I was floating above the house. I couldn't even see the lawn. I thought I saw a star zoom by. But, it wasn't a star. It was a hot air balloon. It had a long, brown streak behind it. Finally, my ride had appeared!

5. Reread the story on Day 4. Why do you think the boy wants to become a squire?

   _____

   _____

   _____

What do you think you would like to do or be when you grow up? Why?

_____

_____

_____

_____

_____

_____

_____

_____

_____

_____

_____

Fluency Blast

Read the passage.

My neighborhood is having a giant yard sale on Saturday. We'll post signs all around town. This week, I'll go through the boxes under my bed. There are many things I know I don't need. At first, my little brother didn't want to help. I told him the money would go to an animal shelter. Then, he was glad to help.

○○○○

Day 1

Jellyfish Lake is a saltwater lake in Palau, an island in the Pacific Ocean. The lake is full of jellyfish. Ocean jellyfish sting, but the golden jellyfish of Jellyfish Lake do not. When visitors swim in the lake, they are surrounded by hundreds of thousands of jellyfish. And, they are all harmless!

1. Where is Jellyfish Lake? _____

2. What is the difference between ocean jellyfish and lake jellyfish? _____
   _____

3. What was the author's purpose in writing this passage? _____
   _____

Day 2

Read the paragraph and circle the adjectives.

A polar bear's white fur makes it hard to see in the white snow. A gecko can disappear on a brown log with its brown, bumpy skin. A striped tiger is hard to see in high grass. Tan lions blend in with the sandy background. Green tree frogs can hide in leafy trees. A leopard with a spotted coat can hide in tall grasses.

Day 3

1. Complete each word with **-oi** or **-oy**.

   v_____ce

   enj_____

   p_____nt

   v_____age

2. Read the word with a short **-oo** vowel sound. Write two more words with the same sound.

   foot   _____ _____

3. Read the word with a long **-oo** vowel sound. Write two more words with the same sound.

   moon   _____ _____

Day 4

Once, the crow was the most beautiful bird in the world. His wings were made of rainbow feathers. One day, it snowed. Rainbow Crow flew far away to get a fire stick from the Great Sky Spirit. The sparks burned Rainbow Crow's feathers. The fire melted the snow, but the crow's feathers had turned black. Then, he looked more carefully. Close up, he could see all of the colors of the rainbow.

1. What kind of story is this? _____

2. What is the moral of this story? _____
   _____

3. What are the three adverbs or adverbial phrases in the story?

   _____ _____ _____

1. Write the adjective(s) that describe each underlined noun.

   <u>Llamas</u> are usually gentle and friendly. _____

   They have big, beautiful <u>eyes</u>. _____

   Llamas have split upper <u>lips</u> like camels. _____

   They have thick wool <u>coats</u>. _____

2. Complete each word with **–oi** or **-oy**.

   "Ah_____," the pirate shouted. "And shiver me timbers, it's you!"

   Mom b_____led eggs to make egg salad.

   An earthquake can destr_____ an entire city.

   My dog jumps for j_____ every day when I come home.

3. Write **L** for each long **-oo** vowel sound (moon). Write **S** for each short **-oo** vowel sound (foot).

   _____spoon   _____took   _____cook

   _____shook   _____tooth   _____stool

4. What is a fable? What is its purpose? _____

   _____

5. Underline the adverbs or adverbial phrases in the passage.

   Rosa flew over the mountains. The air was fast and moved unevenly beneath her wings. She faltered momentarily as her wings tilted to the left. She worried about accidentally falling into a tailspin. Then, a strong breeze turned her sideways. She was safe again!

What is the most fascinating animal you have seen or read about? Explain.

_____

_____

_____

_____

_____

_____

_____

_____

_____

_____

_____

Fluency Blast

Read the passage.

We're having a blizzard. It has been snowing all day. It is also very icy and the roads are dangerous. Earlier, a man crashed right into the back of Mom's car. Mom was upset. But later, we had fun in the snow. We have a huge sledding hill. We went down over and over. We also made a snow family.

○○○○

Day 1

Quicksand is a deep bed of light, loose sand that is full of water. On the surface, quicksand looks much like regular sand. But, it is very different. Regular sand is packed firmly and can be walked on. Quicksand cannot support much weight. People and animals must beware. Quicksand can be deadly.

1. What is **quicksand**? _____
   _____

2. Find a compound word that is used four times in the passage. _____

3. Circle the objects that might float in quicksand.

   bicycle   rock   plastic bag   rake

   car   feather   cow   cotton ball

Day 2

Circle the abstract nouns in each sentence. Underline each concrete noun.

1. I appreciate the honesty in such a young child.

2. On July 4, most Americans show patriotism for their country.

3. The Lee family had a lot of love for each other.

4. The teacher showed compassion to every child.

Day 3

Use context to figure out what the **bold** word means in each sentence. Then, write a short definition.

1. The old man squinted at the words, wishing he had brought his **spectacles**.

   _____

2. The baseball player **writhed** on the ground, holding his broken wrist.

   _____

3. The tea tastes terrible, but if you **dilute** it with water, you can probably drink it.

   _____

Day 4

Koko is homeless. He has wandered too far away from his home and doesn't remember how to get back. His black fur is matted, and his white paws are covered with mud. Koko is afraid of strangers. But, he has found a house to visit. Every morning, he finds a bowl of tuna fish sitting on the porch steps.

1. Which word has a suffix that means **without**?

   _____

2. Is Koko's matted fur tangled or fluffy?

   _____

3. What is Koko's problem? _____

4. How is Koko's problem solved? _____

   _____

1. Reread the passage on Day 1. What is the difference between regular sand and quicksand?

   _____

2. Write the meaning of these compound words based on their parts.

   shipwreck _____

   windshield _____

   motorboat _____

   waterfall _____

3. Write **C** for each concrete noun. Write **A** for each abstract noun.

   _____ peace   _____ armchair   _____ loyalty

   _____ hate   _____ hamburger   _____ hope

4. Use context to figure out what each bold word means. Then, use the word in a sentence.

   I have a fever and chills, so I think I have a bad case of **influenza**.

   _____

   Strep throat can be treated with **antibiotics**.

   _____

5. Write a short definition of each word.

   careless _____

   homeless _____

   Tell about a time you have been sick. What were your symptoms and what helped you get better?

   _____

   _____

   _____

   _____

   _____

   _____

   _____

   _____

Fluency Blast

Read the passage.

Warren sat in front of the TV while a storm raged outside his house. The wind howled, the rain came down in buckets, and thunder boomed loudly. The high winds knocked down a huge oak tree down the street. The tree fell on a power line, cutting off the electricity. Warren found a flashlight and turned it on.

○○○○

Day 1

The 29-day cycle of the moon's phases begins with the new moon. Each night after the new moon, more of the moon appears lighted. This part of the cycle is called waxing. When all of the moon's lighted side faces Earth, it is called the full moon. As the moon cycle continues, we see less of the moon. This is called waning.

1. In which phase of the moon's cycle will you see more of the lit moon? _____

2. Write antonyms for each word.

   waning _____

   waxing _____

3. Which phase is it when all of the moon's lighted side faces Earth? _____

Day 2

Rewrite each sentence correctly. Capitalize the names of books, movies, and song titles.

1. It took Samia only two days to read the book how to be my best friend.

   _____

   _____

2. Gabe and Peter are watching toy store galore for the third time!

   _____

   _____

3. The song "come ride with me" is from my favorite movie.

   _____

   _____

Day 3

1. Complete each word with **–ge** or **–dge**.

   ca_____   ba_____   bri_____   sta_____

2. Circle the correct spelling of the word to complete each sentence.

   The (judge, juge) will make a final decision.

   The lion is stuck on a (lege, ledge).

   You can leave her a (message, massage).

Day 4

Rory climbed the huge sand dune. He was huffing and puffing just like the Big Bad Wolf by the time he got to the top. He looked out over the ocean. Then, he took off his tennis shoes and emptied out the sand. He flopped down on his back and closed his eyes to rest. Before he knew it, he was fast asleep.

1. What fictional character did Rory remind himself of? _____

2. Why do you think Rory fell fast asleep?

   _____

   _____

3. What would be a good title for this story?

   _____

1. Reread the passage from Day 1. Write the two sets of antonyms.

   _____   _____

   _____   _____

2. Rewrite each name of a book, movie, or song with the correct capitalization.

   "a light in the basement" _____

   star city _____

   "pop the cop goes to town" _____

3. Complete each word with **–ge** or **–dge**.

   packa_____   dan_____r   ple_____   fri_____

4. Write three nouns that represent each category.

   pretty   _____   _____   _____

   noisy   _____   _____   _____

5. Write three verbs that could happen in each setting.

   beach   _____   _____   _____

   ranch   _____   _____   _____

Think about a time when you were lost. What happened and how did you feel?

_____
_____
_____
_____
_____
_____
_____
_____
_____
_____
_____

Fluency Blast

Read the passage.

Chase set his canvas backpack on the rock. He wiped the sweat off his face. It was very hot. The sun was hurting his eyes, and the glare was giving him a headache. He wished he had listened to his friends, who said it was too hot in the desert at this time of year. Suddenly, he heard a rattling noise nearby.

○○○○

Day 1

Meteorites are made of bits of rock and metal, so they make quite a crash if they hit Earth. About 50,000 years ago, a million-ton meteorite hit Arizona. It made a bowl-shaped dent in the ground. The **crater** is 570 feet deep and nearly a mile wide!

1. Describe the **crater**. _____

2. Write the correct measurement adjectives in front of each noun.

    _____ years
    _____ meteorite
    _____ feet

3. Why did the author write this passage?

    A. to inform   B. to persuade   C. to entertain

Day 2

Complete each sentence with the correct comparative form of the adjective.

1. I wish it had been _____ during the kite race. (windy)

2. The _____ cheers came at the end of the day when Principal Sneed walked on his hands. (loud)

3. Micah is _____ than Jack, but Jack can sink more basketballs. (tall)

4. The race was _____ between Nadia and Kyle. (close)

Day 3

Use context to figure out what the **bold** words mean in each sentence. Then, write a short definition.

1. I may not be the smartest kid in the class, but my **diligence** gets me As.

    _____

2. I can't help asking questions because I am so **inquisitive** about everything.

    _____

3. Would you say the mullet is one of the more **prevalent** hair styles of the 80s and 90s?

    _____

Day 4

Jenna and her dad made a bluebird house. They made sure the size of the hole was the proper size for a bluebird. That way, the bluebirds could get in, but the house sparrows and starlings could not. Jenna used her dad's hammer to nail it to the side of a porch post. Then, they waited.

1. Why was it important to make sure the hole was the right size?_____

    _____

2. What three birds are named in this passage?

    _____ _____ _____

3. Which two words could be joined to make a contraction? _____ _____

    Write the contraction. _____

1. Write a measurement adjective in front of each noun.

   _____ pizza   _____ yards   _____ weeks   _____ hike

2. Read each word. Then, write the number of syllables in each word.

   _____ adopt   _____ brilliant   _____ diagram

   _____ imitate   _____ journey   _____ predator

3. Write a sentence for each comparative form of **big**.

   _____

   _____

   _____

4. Circle the words in the sentence that can help you define the bold word.

   A **supersleuth**, such as Sherlock Holmes, can help police solve crimes.

   We had to eat a **portion** of everything on our plates, including some peas or broccoli.

   Any form of **precipitation**, such as rain or snow, can make driving dangerous.

5. Write the two words that make up each contraction.

   wouldn't _____ _____   she's _____ _____

   where's _____ _____   hasn't _____ _____

   could've _____ _____   you'll _____ _____

   What sport are you good at? How do you know you are good at it?

   _____

   _____

   _____

   _____

   _____

   _____

   _____

   _____

   _____

   _____

   _____

Fluency Blast

Read the passage.

Ghost towns aren't the strong, lively towns they used to be. Too many people and businesses moved away. Most ghost towns are found in the West. Many used to be thriving mining towns. When nothing was left to mine, the towns dried up. Now, the only people left in the ghost towns are tourists.

○ ○ ○ ○

Day 1

Have you ever seen a UFO? A **UFO** is an unidentified flying object, a strange object or light that people see in the sky. Many people believe that these strange lights are really spaceships from another planet. Some are really airplanes, weather balloons, or meteors. But, many UFO reports are a mystery.

1. Circle the letter of the statement that is a fact.

   A. UFOs are make-believe.

   B. Some UFOs are really airplanes.

   C. People who believe in UFOs are wrong.

2. What does **UFO** stand for? _____

_____

Day 2

Write the verb that agrees with the subject of each sentence.

1. People _____ all kinds of watercraft for pleasure. (use, uses)

2. Some rafts _____ made by tying pieces of wood together. (is, are)

3. Pacific Islanders _____ out tree trunks to make dugout canoes. (digs, dig)

4. The world's largest dugout canoe _____ seven people. (carry, carries)

Day 3

Complete each word with the correct consonant blend.

1. Maria opened her mouth and _____eamed in horror.

2. The _____ain would ruin her shirt!

3. She watched helplessly as it _____ead to her skirt.

4. At least, she thought, it was the same color as her _____othes!

Day 4

Felicia wears a bright red dress with a white sash. On her head is a blue bonnet. It ties under her chin. Her head is made of china, and her shoes are made of real leather. Felicia has lived with the same family for over 200 years. Sadly, her new owner is careless and forgetful.

1. What is Felicia? _____

   Underline the clues that led you to the answer.

2. Which word has a suffix that means **without**?

_____

3. Which word has a suffix that means **full of**?

_____

1. Write **F** for **fact** or **O** for **opinion**.

   _____ UFO stands for unidentified flying object.

   _____ Strange lights in the sky are really spaceships.

   _____ A strange light in the sky could be an airplane or a weather balloon.

   _____ UFOs come from other planets.

2. Match the noun with a verb that agrees with it.

people	cry
corn	hop
kangaroos	sing
skateboards	grows
babies	glide

3. Add a consonant blend to complete each word.

   _____ow   _____ame   _____op

   _____ow   _____ame   _____op

4. Add a suffix to make a new word. Write the definition.

   friend____   _____

   play____   _____

   care____   _____

✏️ **What would you do if a UFO landed in your backyard?**

_____

_____

_____

_____

_____

_____

_____

_____

_____

_____

_____

CD-104979 • © Carson-Dellosa

Fluency Blast

Read the passage.

Tripp and Pablo roller-skated down the sidewalk. Pablo hit a stone and flew forward. His knees and hands slammed hard on the pavement. His head hit the pavement too. It was a good thing he was wearing kneepads. He was glad for his helmet. But, his hands were another story. He wondered how much skate gloves cost.

○○○○

Day 1

Have you ever seen a green, fuzzy spot on bread or cheese? It was probably **mold**. Mold is a type of fungus. The most common molds are green or black. Mold likes to grow in moist, warm places. Foods such as cheese, fruit, and bread can develop mold if left out in warm, damp rooms. It may even grow on leather shoes, belts, or furniture.

1. What is **mold**? _____

2. Find a synonym in the passage for each word.

   usual _____ wet _____

3. Name at least two places where mold grows.

   _____

   _____

Day 2

Choose the correct conjunction to complete each sentence.

1. Do you want to play the violin _____ the piano? (or, but)

2. Mr. Friedman canceled Tasha's lesson _____ he had a cold. (unless, because)

3. Let's play a duet _____ we can learn it in time. (while, if)

4. Liam always practices his scales, _____ April never does. (but, because)

Day 3

Complete each word with the correct consonant blend.

1. It is getting da_____ too early these days.

2. I had not even begun to finish my homewo_____ at 8:00.

3. Dad says I need to thi_____ about my schedule.

4. He thinks I should consider doing my homework fir_____ !

Day 4

Long ago, animals and birds fought battles every day. The bat sat in a tree to see which one won. Then, he would join that side. The chiefs noticed the bat's wishy-washy **character**. They told him that since he was not a real friend to the birds or the animals, he would have to live alone and could fly only at night.

1. What is the main idea of this story? _____

   _____

2. How would you describe the bat? _____

   _____

3. What do you think of the chiefs' punishment?

   _____

   _____

1. Reread the passage on Day 1. Write a synonym from the passage for each word.

   maybe _____   kind _____   grow _____

2. Combine each pair of sentences into one sentence using a conjunction.

   Jack wants to take violin lessons. His sister has been taking them for years.

   _____

   _____

   Nora plays piano by ear. She can't read notes at all.

   _____

   _____

3. Add a consonant blend to complete each word.

   sto_____   sha_____   la_____

   sto_____   sha_____   la_____

4. What does **character** mean? _____

5. Reread the story on Day 4. The bat's character was described as wishy-washy. What other words would describe his character?

   _____   _____   _____

   What are some words that would describe your character?

   _____   _____   _____

   What is the name of your best friend? Describe the characteristics that make him or her your best friend.

   _____
   _____
   _____
   _____
   _____
   _____
   _____
   _____
   _____
   _____

Fluency Blast

Read the passage.

Some stars form pictures or shapes in the night sky. These groups of stars are called constellations. One constellation that is familiar to a lot of people is called The Big Dipper. The Big Dipper looks like a soup ladle. The two stars at the far end of the ladle point to the North Star.

○○○○

Day 1

Brown pelicans like to fish alone. They fly above the water looking for fish far below. When they see fish, they dive down and scoop them up. White pelicans fish together. They also fly high above the water looking for fish. But, when white pelicans find a school of fish, they form a half circle and beat their wings. The **startled** fish swim together and the pelicans dive right in!

1. What is the main idea of this passage?

   _____

2. What does **startled** mean? _____

3. Find a set of antonyms in the passage.

   _____ _____

Day 2

Rewrite the address and the sentence with correct capitalization and punctuation.

1. mr. al rizzo

   _____

   536 foreman road

   _____

   tucson arizona 85712

   _____

2. mother and i went to the atlantic ocean for a day

   _____

   _____

Day 3

Complete each word with the correct consonant blend.

1. Mother put a stack of pancakes on the _____ate.

2. I poured at lea_____ a cup of syrup on them.

3. Mother asked me if I was trying to _____own them in the syrup.

4. I said I just wanted to see if they could _____im.

Day 4

Come here, Thunder, and look!
Come here, Cold, and see it rain!
Thunder strikes and makes it hot.
All seeds grow when it is hot.

1. What is the theme of this Hopi poem? _____

   _____

   _____

2. In the poem, what makes the ground hot?

   _____

   _____

3. What would be a good title for this poem?

   _____

---

1. Reread the passage from Day 1. Draw a Venn diagram to compare the brown and white pelicans.

2. Rewrite the address and the sentence with correct capitalization and punctuation.

   tommy carter   _____

   136 allentown road   _____

   telford pennyslvania 18969   _____

   there are more stars in the milky way galaxy than we can see

   _____

   _____

3. Add a consonant blend to complete each word.

   _____ip   ba_____

   _____ip   ba_____

4. Reread the poem from Day 4. Did you know it was a poem? _____

   Why or why not? _____

   _____

If you could pick a dream vacation to go on, where would it be? Why?

_____

_____

_____

_____

_____

_____

_____

_____

_____

_____

Fluency Blast

Read the passage.

Miguel knew that the family dog down the street had just given birth to puppies. He wanted one in the worst way! He begged his father to let him have one. "You didn't take care of your hamster," Dad told Miguel, "and we had to give him away. What makes you think it will be different this time?"

○ ○ ○ ○

Day 1

Laura Ingalls Wilder is the author of eight books. The first are set in a little log cabin on the edge of the Big Woods in Wisconsin. Then, the family sets out for the prairies of Kansas in their covered wagon. Later, they moved to Minnesota and South Dakota. Her characters and her own family faced many hardships.

1. What is the main idea of this text? _____

_____

2. Where do you think Laura Ingalls Wilder got some of the ideas for her books?

_____

3. Which states did the books take place in?

_____

Day 2

Rewrite the name, address, and sentence with correct capitalization and punctuation.

1. ms teresa small

_____

65 moose lane

_____

homer Alaska 99603

_____

2. the smithsonian museum is in washington dc and it is free

_____

_____

Day 3

Complete each word with **-ar**, **-er**, **-ir**, **-or**, or **-ur** in a way that makes sense in the story.

The f_____mer looked up at the d_____k sky. He looked at the st_____s shining in the sky. The farm_____ saw the N_____th Star. The next m_____ning, he saw a b_____d fly across the sky. The sky is busy, he thought!

Day 4

How beautiful is the rain!
After the dust and heat,
In the broad and fiery street,
In the narrow lane,
How beautiful is the rain!

1. This poem is titled "Rain in Summer" by Henry Wadsworth Longfellow. What could be another title for it? _____

2. List the rhyming words in this poem.

_____ _____ _____ _____

3. How do you think the poet feels about rain?

_____

_____

1. Reread the passage on Day 1. In what kind of home did the characters live? _____
   What do you think that was like? _____
   _____

2. Rewrite the sentences with correct capitalization and punctuation.
   danny can play "three blind mice" on his flute
   _____

   the president lives in the white house on 1600 pennsylvania avenue
   _____

3. Complete each word with **–ar**, **-er**, **-ir**, **-or**, or **–ur**.
   f_____m   b_____n   c_____d
   f_____ m   b_____n   c_____d
   f_____ m   b_____n   c_____d

4. Write two rhyming words for each word.
   growing _____   _____
   height   _____   _____

Describe how you clean your room. List the steps in order.

_____
_____
_____
_____
_____
_____
_____
_____
_____
_____
_____
_____

Fluency Blast

Read the passage.

Most people know this poem. It begins, "Mary had a little lamb. Its fleece was white as snow." The story about Mary and her lamb is told to small children. What most people don't know is the story behind the poem. It was first written for a school song book in 1834!

○○○○

Day 1

The Biggest Trees on Earth

How do redwoods get to be such tall trees? First, they grow where the weather is just right for them. Many redwoods grow near the Pacific Ocean. There, they have hot, dry summers and warm, rainy winters. That means they do not have to try to **survive** during cold weather.

1. Read the title. What does it suggest the passage is about? _____

_____

2. What is the main idea of this passage?

_____

3. What does **survive** mean?

_____

Day 2

1. Choose the verb that agrees with the subject.

Mr. Espinosa _____ his car on Saturdays. (washes, wash)

Aaron and Ali _____ him. (help, helps)

They _____ every inch of the old car with a big sponge. (scrubs, scrub)

Then, they _____ it with soft rags. (polish, polishes)

2. Write a sentence with a subject and a verb. Make sure the verb agrees with the subject.

_____

_____

Day 3

Complete each word by writing its silent letter(s).

1. The little china garden _____nom_____ stood by the path like a little man.

2. You need to brush off the crum_____s from your shirt.

3. I have no dou_____t that you will win an award tomorrow.

4. Mischa has a sprained _____rist from falling off the ladder.

Day 4

Evan loves to read books about insects. His class is in the library. He looks on the shelves where the insect books are usually stacked. None are there. One of the other classes must have checked out all of the insect books to write reports. Evan walks over to the librarian.

1. What do you think will happen next?

A. Evan will check out a book about cars.

B. Evan will ask the librarian if there are any other insect books.

C. Evan will sit down and draw insects.

2. What else could Evan do to solve his problem?

_____

_____

1. Use the word **survive** in a sentence.

   _____

2. Match the noun with a verb that agrees with it.

team	laughs
school	gallops
herd	play
Ms. Gupta	cheers
kittens	closes

3. Complete the words with the correct silent letters.

   thum_____   _____reath   cas_____le   _____not

4. Complete the words with the correct silent letters.

   Jackie ran when she heard the _____nock at the door.

   They studied in a one-room sc_____oolhouse.

   I will _____rite to you every day from camp unless I am busy.

5. Reread the story on Day 4. Write a title for it.

   _____

✎ **Write about the best or worst day of your life.**

   _____

   _____

   _____

   _____

   _____

   _____

   _____

   _____

   _____

   _____

Fluency Blast

Read the passage.

If I were an only child, we would probably eat in restaurants more often. I might be able to join more sports teams. I could watch whatever programs I wanted on TV. I would get all the attention. I could have my own bedroom. And, I would never have to wear hand-me-downs. But, I wonder if I would be lonely!

○ ○ ○ ○

Day 1

Have you ever thought about how great it would be to find sunken treasure at the bottom of the ocean? Kip Wagner is a man who has done just that. He lives in Florida. He knows for a fact that treasure is not only found in storybooks. He has found eight sunken ships. Each one was loaded with gold and silver coins.

1. What is the main idea of this passage? _____
   _____

2. What would be a good title for this passage?
   _____

3. What would you do first if you found a chest full of gold coins? _____
   _____

Day 2

Combine each pair of sentences into one sentence.

1. Bobcats live in the mountains of Virginia. Bears live in the mountains of Virginia.
   _____
   _____

2. The deer drinks from the stream. The coyote drinks from the stream.
   _____
   _____

3. The airplane startled the rabbit. The airplane startled the owl.
   _____
   _____

Day 3

1. Write a synonym for each word.

   shout _____

   angry _____

   lift _____

2. Write an antonym for each word.

   shout _____

   angry _____

   lift _____

Day 4

Today was the day Dylan had been waiting for—his class nature hike. Before the class left, Mrs. Edwards told them that whoever found the most items on the scavenger hunt list would get a prize. Dylan found 16 different leaf **specimens**, or types, and did scratch tests on five different rocks. He was thrilled to win a field microscope!

1. Describe Dylan's attitude. _____

2. What does the word **specimens** mean? _____
   _____

3. Describe the setting the author had in mind when she wrote it. _____
   _____

1. Write two sentences about things you do in school. Then, combine your sentences into one sentence.

   _____

   _____

   _____

2. Circle the synonyms in each sentence.

   I told you to close the door, but you shut the window instead.

   Carla tried to be sure her answers were correct, but not every answer was right.

3. Circle the antonyms in each sentence.

   Did you add to find the answer, or did you subtract?

   Mohammed found it easy to remember the most difficult words.

4. Read the story. Then, compare Danny's experience on the hike with Dylan's in the story on Day 4.

   Today was the day Danny had been dreading—his class nature hike. Danny could barely get out of bed. As if the hike wasn't bad enough, Mrs. Edwards gave the class a list of things to find. Right away Danny lost his canteen. Then, he ripped his T-shirt. He did find a couple rocks, but only because he tripped on them.

   _____

   _____

   _____

   _____

   _____

Describe the people who live in your home and their relationship to you.

_____

_____

_____

_____

_____

_____

_____

_____

_____

_____

Fluency Blast

Read the passage.

Minnie the Mole and her five children live in a cozy den under Mr. Smith's garden. Minnie works hard gathering insects and worms. These are her children's favorite treats. It is not easy being a mole. Moles eat a lot. They eat their own weight in food every day!

○○○○

Day 1

One of the earliest forms of writing was developed in ancient Egypt. The Egyptians used a kind of picture writing called **hieroglyphics**. Today, some museums show examples of hieroglyphics. Language specialists can even read these ancient words.

1. One of the earliest forms of writing was found

   A. in Italy.   B. in France.

   C. in ancient Egypt.   D. in Austrailia.

2. What does the word **hieroglyphics** mean?

   _____

3. Why do you think ancient people tried to find a way to write?

   _____

Day 2

Use coordinating conjunctions (**for, and, or, nor, but, or, yet, so**) to complete each sentence.

1. Do you prefer playing at the park _____ watching TV inside?

2. Mom called me to come in, _____ I pretended I didn't hear her.

3. Kami was tired, _____ she took a little nap.

4. Ian's alarm didn't go off, _____ he was late to school.

Day 3

Choose the correct definition for the bolded multiple-meaning word.

1. Ken's grandparents gave him a **watch** for his birthday.

   A. a small device that tells time

   B. to follow with one's eyes

2. The **pitcher** wound up and threw the ball at the plate.

   A. a container for water

   B. a player on a baseball team

Day 4

Jamal is walking along the edge of the ocean. The surf is pounding and fills his ears. The saltwater spray tickles his face. He licks his lips and notices they taste salty. He never tastes salt on his walks back home. The air feels crisp and cool. The **current** is swift. He watches the waves **break** over his toes. Jamal enjoys the ocean.

1. Underline all the words or phrases that describe how the ocean affected Jamal's senses.

2. What does **break** mean in the context it is used? _____

3. What is another meaning for **break**?

   _____

1. What are hieroglyphics? _____

   The word **hieroglyphics** has _____ syllables.

2. Circle the coordinating conjunctions.

   I had a big dinner, but I'd still like a piece of pie.

   Jim neither went out for basketball nor played any other sports.

   The judges stood up and gave her a standing ovation.

   Lita missed her grandma, so she rode over to see her.

3. Write two sentences, one for each meaning of the multiple-meaning words.

   trunk _____

   trunk _____

   fair _____

   fair _____

4. Read the passage for Day 4 again. What is another meaning for the word **current**? _____

   Use the new meaning in a sentence. _____

   _____

5. What do you like best about the ocean?

   _____

   _____

   _____

Use sensory words to explain how you felt when you went to a memorable birthday party.

_____

_____

_____

_____

_____

_____

_____

_____

_____

Fluency Blast

Read the passage.

Animals get warmth and energy from food. Some animals cannot find enough food in the winter. They must eat large amounts of food in the fall. Their bodies store this food as fat. Then, in winter, they hibernate. Many mammals sleep for five to seven months! Their bodies live on their stored fat.

○○○○

Day 1

Each year, in the fall, doctors have a flu shot for people who want it. The shot helps your body protect itself from several kinds of flu. That way, you are safe if you come into contact with any of those kinds of flu. However, flu **viruses** change quickly. The shot can only protect against the flu viruses it was made for.

1. Read each statement. Write **T** in front of the statements that are true.

____ Everyone must get a flu shot, whether they want it or not.

____ Flu shots are available for people who want them.

____ The flu changes each year, so getting a flu shot every year is good.

Day 2

Use subordinating conjunctions (**if**, **since**, **either**, **or**, **unless**, **because**) to complete each sentence.

1. Mona said she will win the contest _____ she is not too nervous.

2. Lisa wants to go to computer camp _____ she got a new computer.

3. Jose is not going to be in the play _____ someone else drops out.

4. _____ Mom can't drive, someone will have to pick me up.

Day 3

Red is white with black spots. Isn't "Red" a funny name for a dog with that coloring? Red is a fire dog. He lives with the fire chief's family now. The minute the alarm bell rang, he would race to the truck. Red is **not happy** since he **retired**. He misses his working days.

1. What other word could you use instead of **not happy**? _____

2. Use context to figure out what the word **retired** means. _____
_____

3. Why is Red a funny name for the dog in the story?
_____
_____

Day 4

Joanna is crying. She fell on the driveway when her in-line skates hit a stone. Her right knee is cut and bleeding. "Mom!" she calls. Joanna's mother comes out of the house and runs over to Joanna. She looks at Joanna's knee. "Oh my, let's go into the house and take care of that."

1. What do you think will happen next?

A. Joanna's mother will go skating with her.

B. Joanna will throw her skates in the trash.

C. Joanna's mom will help her wash her knee.

2. Write the compound word used in the story.
_____

1. Which definition best fits the meaning of **virus**?

   A. a tiny organism that can make people, plants, or animals sick

   B. a pill that you take in the morning to stay healthy

2. Circle the subordinating conjunctions.

   Joe isn't going to the picnic unless Betsy goes too.

   You should practice every day if you want to get a scholarship.

   Field and track is cancelled today because it is raining.

   Since we live on opposite sides of town, we rarely see each other.

3. Underline the prefix in each word. Write a short definition.

   unafraid _____   uncertain _____

   unstoppable _____   unlatch _____

   What does the prefix **-un** mean? _____

4. Divide each compound word into its two parts.

   eyeballs   backstage   underdog

   meanwhile   raincheck   nowhere

5. Read the passage. What do you think will happen next?

   I saw a wild parrot flying in and out of a tree beside my house. It was beautiful—red and green and white. One day, it flew over to my window sill. I raised the window.

   _____

How do you feel about going to the doctor?

_____

_____

_____

_____

_____

_____

_____

_____

_____

_____

_____

Fluency Blast

Read the passage.

Jeremy was hot from raking leaves. He ran to the kitchen for a glass of water. He didn't notice that his dog's water bowl had overflowed onto the floor. He slipped. As he went down, his arm hit the table. His mother's vase fell and shattered. Oh, no, he thought, there goes the money I earned for raking leaves!

○○○○

Day 1

A lot of people would agree that nothing tastes as good on pancakes or waffles as maple syrup. **Maple syrup** comes from the sap of maple trees. Just before spring comes, the trees send sugar and water up from their roots to their branches. This sugar and water mixture is the sap.

1. Circle the words in this passage that form an opinion.

2. Underline two sentences in this passage that are facts.

3. Where does maple syrup come from?

   _____

Day 2

Circle the correct subordinating or coordinating conjunction.

1. I am neither surprised (but, nor) upset that you didn't go out for hockey.

2. Orlando will only go to practice (if, because) you don't go.

3. Mom only went to PTA meetings (but, for) her children's grades.

4. I will wash the dishes (since, unless) you made dinner.

Day 3

Read the passage aloud, pausing after each sentence. Circle four other words you would pause after.

I rode my bike out the driveway to get the mail. I was anxious to see if I had gotten a postcard from my cousin. My cousin, who was also my best friend, had been away in camp for two weeks. To my great delight, there it was! I sat down on the porch. Then, I read every single word. She was having a good time. And best of all, she would be back soon!

Day 4

I'm a leatherback turtle. Life can be rough for turtles. We have lots of **predators**, including dogs, birds, raccoons, and crabs. They hunt our eggs and babies. Humans hunt us for our shells. They make jewelry and other things from our beautiful shells. It's no wonder we're on the threatened species list!

1. Is this fiction or nonfiction? Explain. _____

   _____

2. What is a **predator**? _____

3. Which word is the opposite of **predator**, prey or carnivore? _____

4. Do turtles have reason to be afraid of humans? Explain. _____

   _____

1. Write **F** for **fact** and **O** for **opinion**.

____ The snow made the backyard look like a winter wonderland.

____ The temperature read 11 degrees!

____ I could not find my mittens.

____ I could not stay warm without my mittens.

2. Write a more interesting synonym for each word.

bad _____   fast _____

slowly _____   pretty _____

3. Circle the coordinating or subordinating conjunction. Write **C** for **coordinating** and **S** for **subordinating**.

____ Mom usually drives me to school, but today I had to take the bus.

____ We can probably get finished if everyone works fast.

____ You can either play basketball with Carlos or take gymnastics with me.

4. Read each sentence. Circle the word(s) you would pause after if you were reading it aloud.

We got up early today, so happy that it was the start of our vacation!

If Brad hadn't yelled out, I would have stepped right on the snake!

Don't you think Charlie should, for once, admit that he was wrong?

5. What is the difference between fiction and nonfiction?

_____

_____

Describe what you would do if you received a case of garlic-flavored gum and were not allowed to throw it out.

_____

_____

_____

_____

_____

_____

_____

_____

_____

_____

Fluency Blast

Read the passage.

Food labels provide a lot of information. They tell how healthy a food is. They say how many calories are in the food. They list what it is made of. Ingredients are listed in order from greatest to least. So, if sugar is listed first, you will know there is more sugar in the food than any other ingredient.

○○○○

Day 1

The Everglades cover about 4,000 square miles of southwestern Florida. Marshes and swamps make up a large part of it. The **tropical** area is hot and wet, which makes it a good home for birds like herons, egrets, and pelicans. There are both crocodiles and alligators. Deer, panthers, otters, and manatees also live there.

1. Why did the author write this passage?

   _____

2. What does **tropical** mean? _____

   _____

3. Of the animals named, which one would you most like to see? _____
   Why? _____

Day 2

Read each sentence. Write **S** for **simple**, **C** for **compound**, and **CX** for **complex**.

____ 1. My dad's car is red and it has white seats.

____ 2. My dad's car is silver.

____ 3. Although my dad's car is gray, it sometimes looks black.

Rewrite each phrase using the possessive form of the plural noun.

4. apples of the tree _____

   _____

5. waves of the ocean _____

   _____

6. pilots of the airplanes _____

   _____

Day 3

Circle the correctly spelled word in each set.

1. beleive   believe   beliefe

2. once   onse   wonse

3. lisence   licencse   license

4. mountan   mountain   montain

5. knock   nock   knoc

Day 4

Gabe and Holly walked down to the water. The sun was setting. The sky blazed in orange, yellow, pink, and red. At the edge of the water sat an odd-looking creature about one foot long. Its body seemed to be in three parts. A long, hard, pointed tail poked out. "Is this a horseshoe crab?" Gabe asked Holly. "I wonder if it will hurt me."

1. What time of day does this story take place?

   _____

2. Where does the story take place? _____

   _____

3. Who are the characters in the story? _____

   _____

1. Use the word **tropical** in a sentence about Florida.

   _____

2. Where would you find another word that means the same as **tropical**?

   A. dictionary   B. thesaurus   C. atlas

3. Write a sentence for each type.

   simple   _____

   compound   _____

   _____

   complex   _____

   _____

4. Cross out the misspelled words and correctly write them above each word.

   My friend Josh was suposed to be here fourty minites ago!

5. A boy and a girl are running. They can see blue sky ahead. There are pebbles on the path. The girl skids and almost falls. She steadies herself on a tree and keeps running. She is not going to give up! She is going to catch the kitten if it's the last thing she does. It is not safe here.

   Where are the boy and girl? Write a setting for this story.

   _____

   _____

What is your opinion of "fast food"? What do you like to order? What healthy options do fast food restaurants offer?

   _____

   _____

   _____

   _____

   _____

   _____

   _____

   _____

   _____

   _____

   _____

Fluency Blast

Read the passage.

Bonnie Butterfly soared through the air. She could see for miles. Bonnie was exhausted and hungry. She wanted to land. She felt comfortable flying, but landing was still a problem for her. She saw a patch of delicious-looking flowers. "Oh dear," she thought, worrying. "Do I dare try to land there?"

○○○○

Day 1

Jane Goodall set up camp in an African jungle near a place where a group of chimpanzees lived. When the chimps saw her, they ran away. They were fearful. But, Jane waited patiently. Eventually, the chimps got used to her. Jane got to know them so well that they became her friends. She even gave them names, such as Fifi, Greybeard, and Grub.

1. What is the passage about? _____
_____

2. What is the setting for the passage? _____
_____

3. How do you think she chose names for the chimps? _____
_____

Day 2

Add punctuation marks where needed.

What do you do when you need to earn extra money Nell and I set up a lemonade stand We made colorful signs to hang around the neighborhood Dad helped us make cookies and chocolate pretzels They were really delicious   Can you guess how much money we made We made over $20 That was a great job

Day 3

Look at the prefixes and their meanings. Then, write two words with each prefix.

1. **pre-**, to do before

_____   _____

2. **re-**, to do again

_____   _____

3. **bi-**, two

_____   _____

4. **mis-**, wrongly

_____   _____

Day 4

My favorite weekend **activity** is going to the library. I like to read more than anything. So, the library is a perfect place for me. I am allowed to take out 10 books each week. After I find my 10 books, I settle down in a beanbag chair. I read as many books as I can before it is time to go home. I think I am a bookworm!

1. Where does this story take place? _____

2. What does the word **activity** mean?
_____

3. Write four compound words in the passage.

_____   _____

_____   _____

1. What do you think about Jane Goodall's life's work? _____
   Why? _____

2. Add punctuation marks where needed.
   Jupiter has at least 63 known moons
   How tall is Mr. Rodriguez
   There's a snake

3. Look at the words you made with prefixes on Day 3. Choose one word and use it in a sentence.

   _____

4. Read the settings below. Briefly describe a story that might happen there.
   ice cold, snow and ice everywhere, warm hut, lake _____
   _____

   palm trees, sand, lifeguards, dolphins jumping out of water _____
   _____

5. Use each word to form a compound word.
   eye   _____
   base   _____
   sweet   _____
   fire   _____

What have you done that you are very proud of? Describe it and tell why you are proud.

_____
_____
_____
_____
_____
_____
_____
_____
_____
_____
_____

Fluency Blast

Read the passage.

Only three problems out of the 32 on his math test were done. For the past half hour, Danny had been looking at the page and daydreaming. He badly needed to pass this test, but he had other things on his mind. "Hey, pass up your paper," Judd said. "Mrs. Walker just asked for our work." Danny froze! ○○○○

Day 1

Almost everyone loves to eat ice cream. Did you know that ice cream has been around for thousands of years? Long ago, Roman rulers enjoyed eating mountain snow. In Europe, people ate ice with added flavors. Later, cream was used to make the kind of ice cream we enjoy today.

1. Which sentence best states the main idea?

    A. Roman rulers ate the mountain snow.

    B. Ice cream has been around for thousands of years.

2. Underline the key detail that best supports the main idea.

3. What was added to ice to form ice cream?

   _____

Day 2

Circle the correct reflexive pronoun to complete each sentence.

1. The basketball star patted (themselves, herself) on the back.

2. We must remind (ourselves, myself) that summer will be here soon.

3. I took a picture of (me, myself) with my phone.

4. Mom wrote (himself, herself) a reminder on the fridge.

5. My brother taught (himself, ourselves) how to swim.

6. The group took (themselves, herself) out of the competition.

Day 3

Look at the suffixes and their meanings. Then, write two words with each suffix.

1. **-er**, one who

   _____ _____

2. **-tion**, state of

   _____ _____

3. **-ness**, condition of

   _____ _____

4. **-able**, able to

   _____ _____

Day 4

Insects kept eating holes in the leaves of George's garden plants. He did not want to use pesticides because they can harm the **environment**. George wanted a solution that would be safe for the environment. He found out that the perfect solution would be ladybugs! These plant guards eat pests but do not damage a garden. He ordered them online!

1. What does **environment** mean? _____

   _____

2. What is George's problem? _____

   _____

3. Complete the effect. Pesticides can harm the environment, so _____

   _____.

1. Reread the passage from Day 1. What sequence of events led up to the ice cream we enjoy today?

   _____

   _____

   _____

2. Complete each sentence with the correct reflexive pronoun.

   He decided to empty the trash _____.

   I will always blame _____ for not remembering her birthday.

3. Use each suffix to make a new word.

   –er _____   –tion _____

   –ness _____   –able _____

4. Circle the cause and underline the effect in each sentence.

   After the chain on the bicycle broke, the wheels would not turn.

   We knew the computer had stopped working when the screen went blank.

✎ **Describe what you collect and why. If you do not collect anything yet, describe what you would like to collect and why.**

_____

_____

_____

_____

_____

_____

_____

_____

_____

_____

Fluency Blast

Read the passage.

Have you ever watched a trained dolphin at an aquarium or water park? Dolphins are believed to be among the smartest animals. There are many kinds of dolphins. The most familiar are the bottle-nosed and the common dolphins. Did you know that the killer whale is actually considered a dolphin?

○○○○

Day 1

Speed skater Bonnie Blair was the youngest in a speed-skating family. She started skating when she was two. Her brothers and sisters were **champions** of skating. They put Bonnie's first skates over her shoes because her feet were so tiny. She trained for years. In 1988, she won her first gold medal at the Olympics. She was the best female speed skater in the world. She was a champion!

1. Why do you think Bonnie started skating at two years old? _____
_____

2. What word in the paragraph is a synonym for **practiced**? _____
What does it mean? _____

Day 2

Circle the word with the correct shade of meaning to complete each sentence.

1. You had better (run, dash, walk) before the big storm hits.

2. My father (shouted, bellowed, screamed) to me to come home.

3. The movie (scared, terrified, frightened) me so badly I had to leave the theater.

4. My cat was (grumpy, cross, furious) with the dog for eating her tuna!

Day 3

Reread the story on Day 1 about Bonnie Blair.

1. What does the word **champion** mean?
_____

How do you know? _____

2. The word **champion** has two meanings. Write a definition for each meaning. Use a dictionary if you do not know them.

noun: _____
_____

verb: _____
_____
_____

Day 4

A Native American **legend** says that a mother bear lay on the beach to watch for her cubs after a fire. Over time, sand covered the bear. Some people still think they can see the shape of a bear sleeping on the beach. This is how the Sleeping Bear Dunes got its name. The dunes are along the shore of Lake Michigan.

1. What kind of story is this text? _____
How do you know? _____

2. What does **legend** mean? _____
_____

3. What is one question you could ask a park ranger at Sleeping Bear Dunes National Lakeshore? _____
_____

1. What do you think most helped speed skater Bonnie Blair get to the Olympics?

   _____

2. Look back to the passage on Day 1 to find the words that are antonyms of these words.

   last _____   huge _____

   worst _____   male _____

3. Place the following sets of words in order from least to most.

   scrub, rinse, clean   _____ _____ _____

   eat, gobble, nibble   _____ _____ _____

   big, enormous, large _____ _____ _____

4. Look back at the two definitions you wrote for **champion** on Day 3. Use each in a sentence.

   _____

   _____

5. How do you think these national parks got their names?

   Grand Canyon _____

   _____

   Crater Lake _____

   _____

What are you afraid of? Why?

   _____

   _____

   _____

   _____

   _____

   _____

   _____

   _____

   _____

   _____

CD-104979 • © Carson-Dellosa

Fluency Blast

Read the passage.

The crowd was in an uproar. The West Bend football team had just made a field goal. The championship game was now tied. Both teams quickly ran off the field. They needed to get advice from their coaches. The crowd waited as November snow drifted down, dusting the noisy stadium with white.

○○○○

Day 1

The night sky is full of treasures. You just have to know where to look. The North Star is easy to find if you live in the Northern Hemisphere. Its star name is Polaris. From the North Pole, the North Star is directly overhead. It is always in the same spot in the sky. Sailors used the North Star to navigate through the oceans.

1. What is the main idea of this passage? _____

   _____

2. Why does the author say, "The night sky is full of treasures"? _____

   _____

3. The name Polaris most likely comes from which name?

   A. polecat   B. polar bear   C. North Pole

Day 2

Circle the correct form of the verb to complete each sentence.

1. Mom _____ extra milk in case of a storm. (buy, bought)

2. The store _____ out of milk before it closed. (sold, sell)

3. We _____ the groceries back to the house. (brought, bring)

4. The TV meteorologist _____ the storm had changed directions. (say, said)

Day 3

Give at least two different meanings for each homonym.

1. bear _____

   _____

2. can _____

   _____

3. bark _____

   _____

4. rose _____

   _____

Day 4

Sally and Norman are swaying slowly in the family swing. The air is crisp. Sally puts her arm around Norman. She snuggles into his shaggy body. Norman's tongue licks her hand. They watch a **sluggish** ladybug crawl underneath a pile of old brown leaves. Norman's graying ears prick up as a southbound V of geese honks good-bye. He barks once at a rabbit.

1. Who are the main characters in this story?

   _____

2. What time of year is it? _____ How do you know? _____

3. What does **sluggish** mean?

   _____

1. Reread the passage from Day 1. Why does the author say, "You just have to know where to look"?

   _____

2. Match the verb to its irregular past tense.

think	met		buy	fed
meet	left		bring	fought
say	thought		fight	lit
fly	flew		feed	bought
leave	said		light	brought

3. Write two sentences to show each meaning of the homonym.

   close

   _____

   _____

4. Reread the story on Day 4. What is Norman? Use words from the text to explain how you know.

   _____

   _____

   _____

5. What time of year is it? Use context clues to find out.

   _____ Jon grew a large pumpkin that might win at the state fair.

   _____ Diana loves picking strawberries, the first fruit of April.

What is your favorite color? Write a letter to your class to persuade them it should be their favorite color too.

_____

_____

_____

_____

_____

_____

_____

_____

_____

Fluency Blast

Read the passage.

It was finally getting cooler. After a blazing hot day, the sun had finally gone down. Abby still couldn't believe their car had broken down. She also couldn't believe her father had decided to walk for help. It was three miles through the desert. The map said there was a town ahead. But, Abby had seen no cars.

○○○○

Day 1

Animal behavior can be a real mystery. One mystery has to do with some animals' strange behavior before earthquakes. Horses and cattle **stampede**. Seabirds screech and dogs howl. Some animals even come out of hibernation early before an earthquake begins.

1. What is the main idea in this passage?

   _____

2. What does the word **stampede** mean?

   _____

3. How do you think these animals know when an earthquake is coming? _____

   _____

   _____

Day 2

Add an apostrophe in each sentence where it is needed.

1. The White Houses address is 1600 Pennsylvania Avenue.

2. Two fires almost destroyed the home of the nations president.

3. Some of the worlds best artists have work displayed in the White House.

4. President George Bushs dogs were named Barney and Miss Beazley.

Day 3

Circle the homophone that correctly completes each sentence.

1. The party is (here, hear).

2. Did you (here, hear) that noise?

3. Randy, you go sit over (they're, their, there).

4. When it cools down, (they're, their, there) going to hike.

5. Sarah and Dad took (they're, their, there) tents down.

Day 4

Chloe's nose was bright red from the cold. She **stomped** the snow off her boots and put them in the mudroom. She set her mittens by the window to dry. Suddenly, Chloe saw that her backpack was open. Her phone was gone! Her heart sank. She had no money for a new phone. Daylight was gone, so she couldn't hunt for it now. If it was in the snow, it was probably already ruined. Now what?

1. What was Chloe's problem? _____

   _____

2. Write two compound words from the story.

   _____   _____

3. What should Chloe do next? _____

   _____

1. Read the words. Write a word that is an opposite, or antonym.

   wide _____ sprinted _____ loud _____ found _____

2. Rewrite each sentence. Replace the underlined words in each sentence with a possessive phrase.

   The hometown of Ronald Reagan was Tampico, Illinois.

   _____

   The nickname of Benjamin Harrison was "Little Ben."

   _____

3. Circle the homophone that correctly completes each sentence.

   We are meeting for lunch an (hour, our) before the movie.

   The 1962 World's Fair was held (hear, here) in Seattle.

   Mei (knew, new) the best way to get to the train station.

4. Write a sentence using both homophones. It's OK if it is a silly sentence.
   dear, deer

   _____

5. Use the word **stomp** in a sentence.

   _____

What do you do to feel better when you are feeling down? How does it help?

_____

_____

_____

_____

_____

_____

_____

_____

_____

_____

_____

CD-104979 • © Carson-Dellosa

Fluency Blast

Read the passage.

   Jawan and I have 40 new shells to add to our collection! We have been scouring the beaches here in Florida. Some shells still had animals living in them. We did not collect those shells. We looked in rock crevices and tide pools. We found a true tulip shell. It is the color of a peach and has an interesting pattern.

○○○○

Day 1

   The **Abominable Snowman**, or Yeti, is a creature that may live on the highest mountain in the world, Mount Everest. Some people believe it is a bear or a gorilla. Others think it is a hairy animal with a body like an ape and a head like a human. There is no clear evidence that the Yeti is real.

1. Why do you think this creature is called the **Abominable Snowman**? _____

   _____

2. What is the highest mountain in the world?

   _____

3. What would make you believe in the Abominable Snowman? _____

   _____

Day 2

Rewrite each phrase using the possessive form of the plural noun.

1. bedroom of the girls _____

2. food of the monkeys _____

3. decisions of the teachers _____

   _____

4. coats of the bears _____

5. fruit of the trees _____

6. milk of the cows _____

7. nuts of the squirrels _____

Day 3

Add a prefix or a suffix to each word. Write the definition of the new word.

_____ cheer_____

_____

_____ agree_____

_____

_____ paint_____

_____

_____ lead_____

_____

_____ treat_____

_____

Day 4

At the end of the day,
Sank the sun in the sky.
The colors were children,
Alive and bright-eyed.

The clouds were the pillows
For each child to rest,
Ready to sleep,
Now so colorfully dressed.

1. What is each section of the poem called?

   _____

2. The clouds are compared to _____.

3. The colors are compared to _____.

1. If there really is an Abominable Snowman, do you think it is friendly or dangerous? _____
   Explain your answer. _____
   _____

2. Replace the words in parentheses with a possessive phrase. Write it on the line.

   The (thick white fur of the polar bears) _____ keeps them warm.

   The (mother of the bear cubs) _____ protects her babies
   from predators.

   The (flippers of seals) _____ make them strong swimmers.

3. Add a prefix or a suffix to the word. Then, use it in a sentence.

   _____art_____

   _____

4. Reread the poem on Day 4. What did the author mean by writing, "The colors were children, Alive and
   bright-eyed?"

   _____

   _____

5. Write a metaphor to describe each word.

   falling leaves _____

   shining star _____

What is your favorite song? Why?

_____

_____

_____

_____

_____

_____

_____

_____

_____

_____

Fluency Blast

Read the passage.

I am going to be in a movie! *The Time Travelers* is being filmed in my town next month. My mom works at the public library. The movie director was asking about our town's history. Mom helped the director. When he saw my photo on Mom's desk, he asked if I might like a small part in the movie. Would I ever!

○○○○

Day 1

As a teen, Jackie Robinson decided to play baseball instead of getting into trouble. It paid off. Soon, he was playing shortstop for the Kansas City Monarchs, a Negro League team. In 1945, professional baseball was still **segregated**. But, in 1947, Jackie started playing with the Brooklyn Dodgers. It was hard at first. But, he soon made Rookie of the Year!

1. What important new fact did you learn?

   _____

2. What does **segregated** mean? _____

   _____

3. Underline the sentence that confirms Jackie was a good player.

Day 2

Rewrite each sentence with correct capitalization.

1. the painting is called *still life: vase with fifteen sunflowers.*

   _____

   _____

2. it was painted in august 1888 by vincent van gogh.

   _____

   _____

3. van gogh was living in arles, france, then.

   _____

4. arles, france, is in europe.

   _____

Day 3

Match each science or social studies word with its meaning.

1. precipitation   a science in which found objects tell about earlier people

2. archeology   the way an animal has changed to survive in its environment

3. adaption   having to do with the entire world

4. global   weather conditions such as snow, sleet, and rain

Day 4

Nathan loved ice fishing with his grandfather on the lake. He watched him chop away at the thick ice. Then, they both dropped their lines through the hole. They sat on their buckets and waited. Suddenly, Nathan's line jerked. He jumped to his feet. He pulled up his line and laughed. The joke was on him. It was not a fish. It was someone's old boot!

1. What is the setting of the story? _____

2. How does Nathan feel about his grandfather?

   _____

3. What did the author really mean when she wrote, "The joke was on him?" _____

   _____

   _____

1. Use the word **segregated** in a sentence.

_____

2. Rewrite the titles of other van Gogh paintings with correct capitalization.

   the starry night _____

   the potato eaters _____

3. Write each word under the subject in which you would study it.

   America   explorer   ecosystem   civilization   species   recycle

Science	Social Studies

4. Read the verbs. Name the setting for each.

   washing dishes, baking smells, refrigerator _____

   sand, blanket, crashing waves _____

5. What does each sentence really mean?

   A light bulb went off over Dan's head. _____

   Keep an eye on the baby. _____

   What would you eat for breakfast if you could have anything? Why?

   _____

   _____

   _____

   _____

   _____

   _____

   _____

   _____

   _____

   _____

   _____

Fluency Blast

Read the passage.

On May 14, 1804, a group of explorers left Saint Charles, Missouri. Thomas Jefferson had hired Meriwether Lewis and William Clark to explore the American West. Jefferson wanted the group to learn about the land, the animals, the plants, and the Native American tribes.

○○○○

Day 1

Glaciers are huge masses of slowly moving ice. Thousands of years ago, they grew very large and covered Earth. As the temperatures warmed, the glaciers started to melt. Huge holes were left where some glaciers used to be. Rain water and melting glacier water filled the holes. Today, some of these "holes" are known as Lake Superior, Lake Michigan, Lake Huron, Lake Erie, and Lake Ontario.

1. What is a **glacier**? _____

2. Complete the effect. Because temperatures warmed, _____ .

3. Complete the cause. Great lakes were formed as a result of _____ .

Day 2

Some words with two or more syllables have a double consonant pattern. Complete the words with a double consonant.

1. a ____ ____ept

2. fli ____ ____er

3. ha ____ ____y

4. pu ____ ____les

5. a ____ ____ition

6. a ____ ____igator

Day 3

Read the sentences aloud. Stop when you come to a word that is incorrect. Correct yourself. Then, write it on the line.

1. The bus stepped at the corner. _____

2. Shannon wanted to eat the beautiful roses.

   _____

3. The baseball player caught the ball with his bat. _____

4. Miguel finished his homework in two bites.

   _____

Day 4

Dear Carolyn,

How's everything in New York? It's been just over a week, but I really miss you! Here in Texas, I am finally able to have a pet. Wiggles is so much fun! He flips his tail when he sees me. He curls into a ball when he sleeps. It tickles when he slithers around my neck.

Love,
Jaime

1. What type of writing is this passage? _____

2. Why do you think she is writing to her friend?

   _____

3. What kind of animal is Wiggles?_____
   What words in the story give you a clue?

   _____

1. Read each cause. Write an effect.

   The chain on Nick's bicycle broke. _____

   The dog jumped out of the tub. _____

2. Read each effect. Write a cause.

   _____. So, Maria took the bus.

   _____. I couldn't go to the movies.

3. Make a list of at least six words with a double consonant pattern.

   _____   _____   _____

   _____   _____   _____

4. Read the sentences aloud. Stop when you come to a word that is incorrect. Correct yourself. Then, write it on the line.

   Eric jumped under the fence. _____

   The American flag waved in the rain. _____

5. Write a more interesting verb to replace the verb in bold.

   Maggie **went** into the empty house. _____

   Jerome **ate** the apple loudly. _____

Imagine that you were going on a jungle animal safari. Think of three things you might say about your first day.

_____

_____

_____

_____

_____

_____

_____

_____

_____

_____

Fluency Blast

Read the passage.

My mom's family owned a bakery. Mom loved the sweet smell of bread and cakes baking in the oven. Every morning, Mom ate a sweet roll for breakfast. She took treats to school for her teachers and friends. Every night, Mom's family ate fresh bread with dinner.

OOOO

Day 1

Before the 1900s, most Americans had never tasted chocolate. But, as far back as 1000 BC, people enjoyed chocolate in a drink. It was made from cocoa beans and bitter spices. Later, people added sugar. In 1828, a Dutch chemist made a powder from the beans called cocoa. Soon, candy makers made candy from cocoa.

1. What was the first chocolate drink made from? _____

2. The authors said most Americans had not tasted chocolate before the 1900s. What do you think happened to change that?

   _____

3. Why was sugar added to the chocolate drinks? _____

Day 2

Change each of the verbs that end in **-y** to the past tense.

1. The mother cat always _____ her kittens in her mouth. (carry)

2. The baby _____ when she was hungry. (cry)

3. Miguel _____ hard at school and got good grades. (try)

4. My dad _____ on me to cut the grass. (rely)

Day 3

Group these words into phrases to help you read the sentences more easily. Circle the phrases. Then, read them aloud.

1. The number of chimpanzees in the wild had been dropping off for decades.

2. The habits of chimpanzees who live in the wild were studied by Jane Goodall.

3. Jane Goodall learned many things in the years she spent with the chimpanzees.

Day 4

Read the letter. Answer the questions.

It was great receiving your letter. Wiggles sounds really cool! I just got a new pet too. Hickory has the softest fur and little pink ears. I love to watch her run on her wheel. But, I won't bring Hickory along when I come to visit. I think Wiggles might like Hickory too much!

1. Infer what kind of animal Hickory is. _____
   What are the clues? _____

2. Wiggles would probably consider Hickory
   A. a new friend.   B. his next meal.
   C. too wild.   D. too scary.

3. What is missing from this type of writing?

   _____

1. Reread the passage on Day 1. Write a title for it.

_____

2. Change each of the verbs that end in **-y** to the past tense.

   try   _____   carry _____

   marry _____   dry   _____

   hurry _____   copy   _____

3. Group these words into phrases to help you read the sentences more easily. Circle the phrases.

   I wish I could bring home a puppy from the shelter.

   Mom rushed off to her job this morning without any breakfast.

4. Write a greeting for a letter to your best friend. Then, write a closing. Use correct punctuation and capitalization.

   greeting _____

   closing   _____

5. Read the descriptions. Infer what kind of animal each one describes.

   black and white, sometimes smelly, stand-up tail _____

   small, green, hops, eats flies, long tongue _____

Name one thing you would like to forget. Explain why.

_____

_____

_____

_____

_____

_____

_____

_____

_____

_____

_____

Fluency Blast

Read the passage.

In the United States, April 22 is Earth Day. On Earth Day, people celebrate the planet Earth. They take the time to remember that the environment is fragile. They also learn what they can do to help save the planet. Some groups plant trees. Others pick up litter. For some caring people, every day is Earth Day! ○○○○

Day 1

In 1875, Daniel Peter and Henri Nestlé began to produce milk chocolate. This took a lot of work and was expensive. It also took a lot of time. In the early 1900s, Milton S. Hershey began to **mass produce** milk chocolate, or make large amounts, at once. The chocolate bars were five cents each.

1. What does **mass produce** mean? _____
_____

2. Why do you think children didn't eat milk chocolate before the early 1900s? _____
_____

3. Have you heard any of the men's names before? Where? _____

Day 2

Use a dictionary to spell the names of these pictures correctly.

_____

_____

_____

Day 3

Use each high-frequency word in a sentence to show that you know what it means.

1. especially _____
_____

2. community _____
_____

3. believe _____
_____

4. whether _____
_____

5. weather _____
_____

Day 4

Jenny put her horses into the barn. Then, she turned to call her two **companions**, Kali and Koko. She heard excited barking where the path met the woods. She called their names, but they continued to bark. Jenny heard a yelp, then total silence. Suddenly, she smelled a terrible **stench** as the two hairy animals ran toward her. She held her nose. They were not coming into the house tonight!

1. What kind of animals are Kali and Koko?
_____ Underline the clues that tell you.

2. What does **stench** mean? _____
What is a synonym for **stench**? _____

3. What does **companion** mean? _____
_____

1. Reread the passage on Day 1. Write a title for it.

   _____

2. Write an antonym for each word.

   scared _____ damp _____ best _____ wealthy _____

3. Use a dictionary to spell the names of these pictures correctly.

   _____   _____   _____

4. Choose the correct high-frequency word to complete the sentence.

   My mother is (especially, specialty) proud of her red velvet cake.

   The police do a lot of good deeds in the (communion, community).

   Carmen didn't know (weather, whether) to laugh or cry.

5. What animal is it? Use context clues to find out.

   _____The huge mammal blew a big puff of water from its spout.

   _____The baby jumped out of its mother's pouch and hopped away.

   _____The gray rodent stuffed nuts into its cheek pouches and ran away.

   If you could fly, where would you go? Why?

   _____
   _____
   _____
   _____
   _____
   _____
   _____
   _____
   _____
   _____
   _____
   _____

Fluency Blast

Read the passage.

Eyeglasses can help people in different ways. Some people cannot see things far away. Those people are nearsighted. Some people cannot see things close to them. Those people are farsighted. Glasses can be worn to help either problem. See an eye doctor when you need help.

○○○○

Day 1

Native Americans have used **herbs** and other plants as medicine for many years. Garlic cloves soothe insect stings. Pinesap heals cuts. Sunflowers can soothe a blister. Dandelion tea is good for heartburn. Willow bark can cure a headache. Today, many of these herbs are available in drugstores.

1. Which letter is silent in **herb**? _____

2. What can be used as medicine for a headache? _____
   Insect stings? _____

3. What was the author's purpose for writing this passage?

   A. to entertain   B. to inform   C. to persuade

Day 2

Describe the characterstics of a person who is:

1. helpful _____
2. friendly _____
3. careful _____
4. happy _____
5. fearless _____
6. talkative _____
7. speedy _____

Day 3

Write words that end in **–ight**. Use each one in a sentence.

1. ____ight _____
   _____

2. ____ight _____
   _____

3. ____ight _____
   _____

4. ____ight _____
   _____

Day 4

A starfish washes up by Jayla's toes. A little farther down, she spies a sand dollar and several pale seashells. Jayla puts the starfish, sand dollar, and all of the shells she collected in a bucket. She is thrilled. She loves to vacation with her family.

1. Where do you think Jayla is? _____
   Underline the clues that tell you.

2. Why do you think Jayla put her finds in a bucket? _____
   _____

3. Write the compound words used in the passage.

   _____   _____

1. Which letter is silent in each word?

   knob ____   gnat ____   wrap ____   lamb ____

2. Complete each sentence.

   A person who is cheerful _____.

   A person who is forceful _____.

   A person who is orderly _____.

3. Write words that end in **-ought**. Then, write a short definition for each word.

   ____ ought   _____

   ____ ought   _____

4. Write three compound words. Divide them into their parts.

   _____

   _____

   _____

5. Write an antonym for each word.

   whole   _____

   jolly   _____

   question   _____

   remember _____

Which animal do you wish could talk to you? What questions would you ask it?

_____

_____

_____

_____

_____

_____

_____

_____

_____

_____

    CD-104979 • © Carson-Dellosa

Fluency Blast

Read the passage.

Today was the first day of Biscuit's obedience class. We arrived before most of the other dogs and owners. Biscuit sniffed and greeted the dogs as they approached. She wagged her tail cheerfully. Biscuit was a quick learner and picked up the commands right away. I was proud. She will earn her diploma in no time! ○○○○

Day 1

There are two kinds of boomerangs. Returning boomerangs are flat, curved objects that spin through the air and return. The cave dwellers made non-returning boomerangs. They were thrown in a straight path. They were valuable hunting weapons because they could spin through the air and hit a target harder than a stick or stone.

1. To what type of boomerang does "spin through the air and return" refer?

   _____

2. Why were non-returning boomerangs valuable? _____

   _____

   _____

Day 2

Determine the meaning of each word based on the meaning of the affix.

1. preheat _____

2. uncomfortable _____

3. painless _____

4. dislike _____

5. midfield _____

6. mindful _____

7. wonderment _____

8. pointless _____

Day 3

Circle the correctly spelled word in each set.

1. becase   becaus   because

2. Wendsday   Wensday   Wednesday

3. friendly   freindly   frendly

4. pleese   please   plaese

5. excus   excuse   xcuse

Day 4

Hector and Jai were walking home through the woods behind the school. Suddenly, they noticed many squirrels running in the same direction. Hector and Jai followed them to a clearing. They saw hundreds of squirrels! They stared in amazement. One plump squirrel **skittered** over to them and said, "Would you care to join us for lunch?"

1. What genre is this passage?

   A. poetry   B. fiction
   C. biography   D. fable

2. Underline the clue in the passage that tells you what genre this is.

3. What does **skittered** mean? _____

   _____

1. What happens when you throw a returning boomerang?

   _____

2. Divide the words into syllables.

   centipede   butterfly   grandmother   misunderstand

3. Complete each sentence with the correct word.

   My shoe is _____, so I hope I don't trip on the lace. (tied, untied)

   Will _____when his parents are not looking. (behaves, misbehaves)

   Tyler won't eat his peas because he _____ them so much. (likes, dislikes)

4. Cross out each misspelled word and write the correct spelling above it.

   Chocolate is my favrite kind of ice craem. I could eat it for ever meal, not just for desert. It is too

   bad my perents don't agree with me!

5. Reread the story on Day 4. Write a title for it.

   _____

✏️ **What would be the first thing you would do if you were invisible? Why?**

_____
_____
_____
_____
_____
_____
_____
_____
_____
_____
_____

Fluency Blast

Read the passage.

Mammals are warm-blooded animals. Most mammals have hair on their bodies. Many of them live on land. People, elephants, rabbits, dogs, and cats are all land mammals. Dolphins and whales are mammals that live in water. The seal, walrus, and otter are mammals that live on land and in the water.

○○○○

Day 1

For almost 400 years, people have made mirrors from plate glass. The front of the glass is polished. The back is painted with a **substance** that reflects light. The glass is then cut into many sizes. A flat mirror reflects a correct image. If the mirror is wavy or curved, the image will look odd. That is why people look so funny in carnival mirrors.

1. Use a word from the text to fill in each blank.

   A flat mirror reflects a _____ image.

   If the mirror is _____, the image will look odd.

   People look funny in _____ mirrors.

2. What was the author's purpose for this text?
   A. to entertain   B. to inform   C. to persuade

Day 2

Complete the sentences with the correct comparative adverb.

1. Over the summer, Mia grew _____ than Jane. (tall, taller, tallest)

2. Of all of my brothers, I grew the _____. (tall, taller, tallest)

3. Kim sang _____ than any other girl in the choir. (more beautifully, most beautifully)

4. Aunt Bea read to us _____ than Uncle Calvin. (more slowly, most slowly)

Day 3

Read the passage two times. Then, answer the questions.

The alarm rang quietly. I jumped off the floor. It was midnight and I was already late for dinner. I threw on my pajamas and ran over the sidewalk. If I slowed down a bit, I might get there late.

1. Does it sound right? _____

   Why not? _____

   _____

2. Does it make sense? _____

   Why not? _____

   _____

Day 4

A little nose poked out of Daysha's backpack. She quickly warned the **alien** to get back inside before someone saw it. The alien's name was Jogi. She had asked if Jogi was a boy's or girl's name, but Jogi did not understand. Now, they were on their way to school, another thing Jogi had never heard of. What a strange, new world!

1. What was the author's purpose for this text?
   A. to entertain   B. to inform   C. to persuade

2. What is Jogi? _____

3. What would you do if an alien appeared one night in your bedroom? _____

   _____

   _____

1. Use the word **substance** in a sentence.

   _____

2. Write sentences using the words **funny**, **funnier**, and **funniest**.

   _____

   _____

   _____

3. Reread the text from Day 3, shown below. Underline the words and phrases that do not sound right or do not make sense.

   The alarm rang quietly. I jumped off the floor. It was midnight and I was already late for dinner. I threw on my pajamas and ran over the sidewalk. If I slowed down a bit, I might get there late.

4. Reread the passage from Day 4. Is it fiction or nonfiction? _____

   Underline the clues that tell you.

5. Reread the story on Day 4. Write a title for it.

   _____

Compare what it would be like to be a snowflake after having been a raindrop all of your life.

_____

_____

_____

_____

_____

_____

_____

_____

_____

Fluency Blast

Read the passage.

Tomas looked at the animals waiting for a new home in the shelter. He wanted to rescue a cat today. But, how was he to choose? As he walked by the cages, he noticed that a yellow tabby kept reaching out her paw to him as he passed. "Are you choosing me?" he asked, smiling. He called the attendant.

○○○○

Day 1

Animals in the desert are different from those that live in other regions. The Gila monster, a **venomous** lizard, spends most of its time underground. It can go for months between meals. The javelina is a wild pig. It has a tough mouth and stomach. This helps it eat cactus plants with sharp spines.

1. What does **venomous** mean?

   _____

2. Underline the main idea of this passage. List two supporting details.

   _____

   _____

   _____

Day 2

Circle the word that makes the most sense in the sentence. Then, explain your choice.

1. The fish was so (big, large, gigantic) it didn't fit in the pan.

   _____

2. Mr. Walker was (mad, angry, furious) at the substitute for skipping the lesson.

   _____

3. Sherry was (glad, happy, ecstatic) that she won a free trip to the moon.

   _____

Day 3

Make new words by adding each prefix or suffix to the base word.

1. happy (un-, -ness, -er)

   _____ _____ _____

2. agree (dis-, -ment, -able)

   _____ _____ _____

3. pay (pre-, -er, -ment)

   _____ _____ _____

4. heat (pre-, -ing, -er)

   _____ _____ _____

Day 4

At 5:05 pm, we were called to the home of a Mr. and Mrs. Bear. They had been out all day. When they got back, they found the lock on their door was broken. Officer Paws and I found that food had been stolen and a chair had been broken. When we went upstairs, we found a female human asleep in a small bed. She claimed her name was Goldilocks. The Bear family did not know her.

1. Does this police report remind you of another story you know? _____ Which one?

   _____

2. What would be a good title for this story?

   _____

1. Use the word **venomous** in a sentence.

   _____

2. Write two more words to show shades of meaning from least to most.

   hop   _____   _____

   pretty   _____   _____

   funny   _____   _____

3. Make new words by adding each prefix or suffix to the base word. Then, write definitions for the new words.

   like (dis-, -able, -ly)

   _____   _____

   _____   _____

   _____   _____

4. Underline the verbs in each sentence. Write **P** for present tense and **PT** for past tense.

   _____ Scotty begs for a treat every day.

   _____ Mari wanted to shop for new jeans.

   _____ I can only play one game at a time!

5. Write the number of syllables in each word.

   _____ punish   _____ scream   _____ distance   _____ navigate

   _____ butterfly   _____ highway   _____ migrate   _____ reached

   Write a poem about your favorite person, place, or animal.

   _____

   _____

   _____

   _____

   _____

   _____

   _____

   _____

   _____

   _____

   _____

Fluency Blast

Read the passage.

Reports of strange things falling from the sky have been floating around for over 100 years. People have seen small frogs, fish, grasshoppers, and snails drop from the sky. They saw them in places like France, India, and the United States. Even stranger, in 1995, it rained soda cans in the Midwest!

○○○○

Day 1

Wolves are the wild relatives of dogs. They live in family groups. Scientists say that wolves communicate, or talk, with each other. They use howls, noises, and movements. The wolves use their voices, and their bodies pass on important information.

1. What is the main idea of this passage?

   _____

2. What synonym for **talk** is used in the text?

   _____

3. What do wolves use to communicate? _____

   _____

   _____

Day 2

These sentences cannot be taken literally. Underline the nonliteral words. Then, write the real meaning of each sentence.

1. The test was a piece of cake.

   _____

   _____

2. Our car is on its last legs.

   _____

   _____

3. Will you give me a hand?

   _____

   _____

Day 3

Choose **–tion** or **–sion** to correctly complete each word.

1. lo_____

2. ten_____

3. cau_____

4. permis_____

5. man_____

6. frac_____

7. discus_____

8. pollu_____

Day 4

Ralph was a dirty mutt. His once-white hair was gray with grime. Around his dirty collar was an old identification tag. Ralph's bright, black eyes were glued to a plate at the edge of the table. On it was a ham sandwich. Ralph knew he would get chased away if the lady of the house caught him again.

1. What kind of dog is Ralph? _____

2. Does Ralph live with the lady of the house?____
   How do you know? _____

   _____

3. Did Ralph have a home at one time? _____
   Explain your answer. _____

   _____

1. Use the word **communicate** in a sentence.

   _____

2. What are three synonyms for the word **talk**?

   _____   _____   _____

3. What are the literal and nonliteral meanings of each sentence?

   She's a couch potato.

   Literal: _____

   Nonliteral: _____

   He was all ears.

   Literal: _____

   Nonliteral: _____

4. Circle the correct spelling of each word

stasion	adoption	plantasion	exhausion
station	adopsion	plantation	exhaustion

5. Reread the story on Day 4. What do you think happened next?

   _____

   _____

   _____

What is your favorite time of day? Why?

_____

_____

_____

_____

_____

_____

_____

_____

_____

_____

_____

CD-104979 • © Carson-Dellosa

Fluency Blast

Read the passage.

Norman Rockwell lived from 1894 until 1978. He was a popular artist. He drew pictures for pages of children's magazines. He is most famous for painting pictures of everyday life in small towns. He called himself a storyteller. That's because of the stories his paintings told about families and neighbors.

○○○○

Day 1

Bacteria are among the smallest forms of life but do many things. They are made of only one cell. They can only be seen with a microscope. Some bacteria can be helpful. For example, bacteria can help people digest certain foods. They are used in making cheese and vinegar. Other bacteria can be harmful. Certain bacteria cause **diseases**. Bacteria can also cause food to spoil.

1. Name one thing bacteria can be useful for.

   _____

2. Write two words from the passage that are antonyms. _____ _____

3. What is the main idea of the passage? _____

   _____

Day 2

Use a thesaurus to find two synonyms for each word.

1. clean _____ _____

2. easy _____ _____

3. fast _____ _____

Use a dictionary to find the meaning of each word.

4. expand _____

   _____

5. negotiate _____

   _____

Day 3

C makes both a **soft /s/** and a **hard /k/** sound. Write the words in the correct spaces.

circus	cable	nice	cereal
candle	castle	recess	

1. soft c _____

   _____

2. hard c _____

   _____

3. both _____

   _____

Day 4

It's tough being a turtle. I'm on the threatened species list. Some humans make our lives difficult. They hunt us for our shells! They use them to make jewelry. Some people eat turtle meat and eggs. People also drive across turtle paths. And, there are so many of them on our beaches. But, not all is doom and gloom. Other people are working to save us. I think they'll win!

1. What is the problem of the turtle in the story?

   _____

2. Underline the sentences that are opinions. Circle the sentences that are facts.

3. Which two words in the text have three syllables? _____

   _____

1. Reread the passage on Day 1. Write one fact about each word.

    bacteria _____

    disease _____

2. Use a thesaurus to find two synonyms for each word.

    cold   _____   _____

    begin   _____   _____

    small   _____   _____

3. Write **S** for soft **c** and **K** for hard **c**.

    _____ certain   _____ comb

    _____ corn   _____ pencil

    _____ camel   _____ juice

4. The topic is wild animals. State one opinion. State one fact.

    opinion _____

    fact _____

5. Circle the words that have three syllables.

    understand   certain

    holiday   envelope

    purple   evergreen

Write about a time when you or someone else was a good neighbor.

_____

_____

_____

_____

_____

_____

_____

_____

_____

_____

 CD-104979 • © Carson-Dellosa

Fluency Blast

Read the passage.

A topiary is a kind of sculpture made from plants, usually shrubs or trees. Topiaries are cut to resemble many different things. Some are shaped like animals. For example, a topiary can look like an elephant, a bear, a horse, or even a dinosaur. Others are trimmed to look like castles, cones, or mazes.

○○○○

Day 1

Fingernails and toenails are made from cells of hard skin. They guard the ends of your fingers and toes. Nails grow from the base to the tip. Each nail has a light half-moon shape at its base. Your nail starts to grow from this area. It takes about six months for nails to grow from base to tip. Fingernails grow faster than toenails.

1. What is the main idea of this passage?

   _____

2. How do nails grow?

   _____

3. What are nails made of?

   _____

Day 2

Place the sentences in the correct order.

_____ That is because she was always popping up and down.

_____ So, we named her Chase instead.

_____ We were going to name the cat Gopher.

_____ Then, we saw her chase a gopher out of the lawn.

_____ We got a new cat from the adoption center.

Day 3

Divide each word between the syllables. Write **O** for open or **C** for closed to identify each syllable.

1. h u m a n

2. h a p p y

3. s i l e n t

4. d e n t i s t

5. a p r o n

Day 4

The wind blew softly, rippling the grasses across the prairie. The sun was bright. Anna was glad for the shade of her sunbonnet. She placed the iron pot on the fire. She stirred the stew, then climbed into the covered wagon to find the tin plates and cups. She knew Pa would want his lunch when he returned.

1. The story most likely takes place
   A. in the past.
   B. in the present.
   C. in the future.

2. What is the time of day? _____

3. What is the setting of the story? _____
   _____

1. Reread the passage on Day 1.

   What did you already know before reading it?

   _____

   What did you learn that you did not know before?

   _____

2. Add another word to each word to make a compound word.

   sand_____

   every_____

   wood_____

   up_____

   boat_____

3. Place the sentences in the correct order.

   _____ First, we went downtown to watch the parade.

   _____ Yesterday was the Fourth of July.

   _____ Finally, we watched fireworks from the roof of our house.

   _____ Then, we went to the park and had a picnic.

4. Divide each word between the syllables. Write **O** for open or **C** for closed to identify each syllable.

   s a d d e r   h o t e l   p r e t e n d   n a p k i n

What is the best thing about being a kid? Why?

_____

_____

_____

_____

_____

_____

_____

_____

_____

_____

_____

Fluency Blast

Read the passage.

Brianna and her mother wanted to plant a garden for butterflies. They found out that butterflies must eat in the larval stage. So, a butterfly garden needs the right kind of food for that stage. And, they wanted the butterflies to stick around. So, they also needed to plant food for adult butterflies.

○○○○

Day 1

An unusual animal **mystery** involves birds and ants. No one can explain why birds do this. But, birds have often been seen to pick up an ant in their beaks and then rub it over their feathers again and again. This is called "anting." Birds have been observed doing this for an hour without stopping!

1. What does the word **mystery** mean?

   _____

2. What is the main idea of this passage?

   _____

3. Which two words are synonyms?

   _____   _____

Day 2

Underline the time-order words in the passage.

I rarely go to the library on Saturday. But today, I decided I needed something to read for tomorrow. Then, I will be sitting at an airport. My mother is finally coming home from China. Afterward, we will go out for ice cream. Finally, we will relax at home. Immediately, it will be as if she had never been away.

Day 3

Use each base word to create two new words.

1. graph

   _____

   _____

2. scope

   _____

   _____

3. phone

   _____

   _____

Day 4

When we first climbed into the car and snapped on our safety belts, I wasn't nervous. But, as we started to descend the hill, my heart skipped a beat. Soon, we were going downhill fast! With a twist, a loop, and a bunch of fast turns, everyone on board screamed in delight.

1. What is the setting of this passage? _____

   _____

2. Is the passage written in first person or third person? _____

3. What does the idiom "My heart skipped a beat" mean?

   _____

   _____

1. Reread the passage on Day 1. Why do you think birds can be seen "anting"?

_____

_____

2. Write a synonym for each word.

infant _____   shout _____

speak _____   incorrect _____

afraid _____   adore _____

3. Complete each sentence with an appropriate time-order word. The sentences are in order of the story.

_____, I woke up on the wrong side of bed.

_____, I had to make my own breakfast.

_____, I missed the bus.

_____, I was late to school and missed a test. What a day!

4. Use each base word to create one or more new words.

port _____

aqua _____

view _____

Explain a difficult decision you had to make.

_____

_____

_____

_____

_____

_____

_____

_____

_____

_____

Fluency Blast

Read the passage.

When you think of delicious berries, you probably think of strawberries, blueberries, and raspberries. You probably don't ever think to snack on cranberries. Cranberries are tart berries used in relishes, sauces, and desserts. Cranberries also make a delicious juice that is very healthy.

○○○○

Day 1

The "land of opposites" is a good nickname for the desert. Temperatures can go from one extreme to the other. It is often scorching hot during the day. At night, freezing cold temperatures may move in. The **precipitation** in the desert also varies greatly. For months, it may be dry. Suddenly, the floods come.

1. What does **precipitation** mean?

   _____

2. Give three examples of precipitation.

   _____ _____ _____

3. Which adverb tells how hot it is? _____

4. Which adverb tells how cold it is? _____

Day 2

Circle the word in each line that does not belong in the set of words.

1. gold   silver   yellow   bronze

2. quickly   slowly   rapidly   correctly

3. week   hour   second   minute

4. cry   smile   laugh   enjoy

Day 3

G makes both a **soft /j/** and a **hard /g/** sound. Write the words in the correct spaces.

garage	engine	goal
game	baggage	giant

1. soft g _____

   _____

2. hard g _____

   _____

3. both _____

   _____

Day 4

Underneath the magical Silver Cord Waterfall is the secret and mysterious Crystal Cave. There lived a village of animals. A kind, old man created it for the animals during a great forest flood. With a wave of his wand, the man **granted** a special power to each animal to help it escape the rising waters.

1. What was Silver Cord? _____

2. What does **granted** mean? _____

3. Which word in the passage is a synonym for **town**? _____

4. What magic was the old man able to perform?

   _____

   _____

1. Use the word **precipitation** in a sentence.

   _____

2. Circle the word in each line that does not belong.

rain	cold	snow	sleet
window	glass	sink	mirror
mile	yard	minute	meter
happy	smile	sad	angry

3. Write **J** for soft **g** and **G** for hard **g**.

   _____ goose   _____ gym

   _____ gel   _____ imagine

   _____ gifts   _____ gingerbread

4. Reread the passage for Day 4. After each animal's name, write a power it might have received to save it from the flood.

   giraffe   _____

   great ape   _____

   lion   _____

5. Reread the story on Day 4. Write a title for it.

   _____

If you had the chance to go into outer space, would you go? Why or why not?

_____
_____
_____
_____
_____
_____
_____
_____
_____
_____
_____

Fluency Blast

Read the passage.

Michelle looked on the internet. She found a good website. It showed pictures of Mars. They were taken by spaceships that had landed there. The photos showed the planet's volcanoes, canyons, and channels. Michelle wondered if she would ever see this planet on her own.

○○○○

Day 1

Many African Americans have led the way through history. Jackie Robinson was the first African American to play major league baseball. Matthew Henson was an early explorer of the North Pole. Benjamin Banneker helped design the city of Washington, DC. Guy Bluford was an astronaut. Shirley Chisholm was an elected congresswoman.

1. What is one thing each of these people have in common?

_____

2. Who went to the North Pole?

_____

3. Who was an elected congresswoman?

_____

Day 2

Circle the double negative in each sentence. Rewrite one of the sentences correctly.

1. There were not no oranges on the tree.

2. Juan never saw nobody he knew at the mall.

3. None of the students weren't born in another country.

_____

_____

Day 3

Write the correct definition for each bolded homograph.

1. The **wind** is blowing hard today.

_____

2. Grandfather stopped to **wind** his watch.

_____

3. The violinist made a low **bow** to the crowd.

_____

4. I had a hard time tying a **bow** on this gift!

_____

Day 4

Irina was at her computer. She had to write a paper for her science class. Mr. Lee assigned each person a different topic. Irina's assignment was carnivorous plants. Irina looked up the word **carnivorous**. She gasped! Mr. Lee must have been joking. Surely, there was no such thing. When she googled it, she got over two million results!

1. What was Irina's homework assignment?

_____

_____

2. What does **carnivorous** mean? Look it up if you don't know.

_____

1. Reread the passage on Day 1. Name one African American leader and describe his or her claim to fame.

   _____

2. Circle the word or words that correctly complete each sentence.

   The jellyfish don't (never, ever) stop moving.

   They don't do (anything, nothing) but follow the sun all day.

   People who swim with jellyfish shouldn't (ever, never) lift or throw them.

   There (was, was not) no need for jellyfish to have stingers.

3. Write the two definitions of each homograph.

   desert _____
   desert _____
   row   _____
   row   _____

4. Two other forms of the word **dress** are **dresser** and **dressing**. Write a sentence using all three. It's OK if it is a silly sentence.

   _____
   _____

If you had one thousand dollars to give to a charitable cause, which one would you choose? Why?

_____
_____
_____
_____
_____
_____
_____
_____
_____
_____

CD-104979 • © Carson-Dellosa

Answer Key

Page 9
Day 1: 1. Their homes, called hogans; 2. A hogan is a home made of wood and mud. 3. to let the sunlight in; 4. southwestern; **Day 2:** 1. I; 2–3. Answers will vary. **Day 3:** 1. (underlined) dis-, re-; 2. (circled) –ly, -ed, -ful, -ly, -ly; 3. (left to right) 2, 3, 2, 2; **Day 4:** 1. city, It is an apartment building and has a playground. 2. The hogan is a single home made of mud and wood. The other home is in an apartment building with other families. They both are places where people live.

Page 10
1. (circled) toothpick, lipstick, bookmark, runaway; 2. Answers will vary. 3. un-/-able, pre-/-er, dis-/-ful, re-/-ing; 4. They are both about homes. The homes are made differently and are in different places. 5. beautiful, back, there, play, my, best

Page 11
Day 1: 1. a celebration; 2. Japan; 3. April; 4. outside; **Day 2:** 1. He, her; They, them; 2. brought, think, spoke, meant; **Day 3:** 1. of the physical surroundings; 2. She forgets to set her alarm. 3. Answers will vary. **Day 4:** (underlined) Pitter and Patter are two drops of water. 2. when two or more people meet again; 3. Water falls onto the earth, later evaporates into the air and forms clouds.

Page 12
1. Answers will vary. 2. his, them, her, my; 3. catch/caught, bite/bit, leave/left, throw/threw, stick/stuck, fly/flew; 4. Answers will vary.

Page 13
Day 1: 1. of the sun; 2. The sun's light is blocked from Earth when the moon passes between them. 3. He thinks they are amazing events. **Day 2:** 1. Jacques Cousteau explored many of Earth's oceans. He believed it was important to protect ocean life. He created a group called the Cousteau Society. More than 50,000 people belong to it today.

Day 3: 1. fantastic; 2. remember; 3. telephone; 4. hamburger; 5. vitamins; **Day 4:** 1. Jason's; 2. fiction, because it would not happen in real life; 3. Answers will vary.

Page 14
1. Answers will vary. 2. to inform; 3. (circled) do, loch, ness, she, Nessie; question mark after monster, period after Nessie; 4. el/e/phant, ac/ro/bat, grav/i/ty, la/dy/bug, mul/ti/ply; 5. Answers will vary.

Page 15
Day 1: 1. noise; 2. unpleasant sounds; 3. pleasant/unpleasant; 4. harmful/dangerous; **Day 2:** 1. (circled) yesterday/fell; 2. easily/caught; 3. outside/play; 4. over/boiled; **Day 3:** 1. (underlined) dis-, over-, non-; 2. (circled) -ment, -ing, -ly, -ing; 3. 6, 4, 4, 2; **Day 4:** 1. Anita, Miguel; 2. someone from another place or family; 3. They were wide open.

Page 16
1. Answers will vary but may include begin, easy, look, odd. 2. Answers will vary but may include add, backward, dull, tight. 3. (circled) slowly, yesterday, outside; 4. un-/-able, pre-/-er, dis-/-ful, re-/-ing; 5. They listen to everything.

Page 17
Day 1: 1. the Canadian Arctic; 2. frozen lake in the Canadian Arctic; 3. the ice must be frozen thick; **Day 2:** 1. (circled) Saturday, July, Lily's, Lily, Mom, Lily, Mom, Grandpa Henry, Lily, Gabe, Tamiko, Eliza, Ben; periods after birthday, fun, movies, popcorn, shakes, arrive; **Day 3:** 1. especially; 2. beautiful; 3. impossible; 4. people; **Day 4:** 1. Mario made patties. Mario sprinkled salt and pepper on them. He turned them over. 2. Answers will vary.

Page 18
1. to inform; 2. Michelle Wie's family is Korean. Memorial Day and Labor Day always fall on a Monday. 3. Saturday, July 4; Thursday, September 18; Friday, December 23; 4. (crossed out/corrected) rite/right, liberry/library, wite/white; 5. Answers will vary.

Answer Key

Page 19
Day 1: 1. An arachnid has four pairs of legs and two body parts. 2. They trap insects in webs. 3. sticky; **Day 2:** 1. quotation marks placed before I and after Italy, before I and after English, before My and after English, before But and after speak! 2. France, Louie, French, English, Sarah, Kate, Australia; **Day 3:** 1. (circled) break; 2. (circled) said; 3. (circled) grown; 4. (circled) rough; 5. (circled) lawyer; **Day 4:** 1. 8; 2. excited; 3. a servant; 4. a contest

Page 20
1. quotation marks placed before This and after lessons, before Our and after attic, before I and after day; 2. Answers will vary. 3. ea, aw, ou, ai, ow; 4. (circled) dream, floating, house, lawn, brown, streak, appeared; 5. Answers will vary.

Page 21
Day 1: 1. Palau; 2. Ocean jellyfish sting and these jellyfish do not. 3. to inform; **Day 2:** (circled) polar, white, white, brown, brown, bumpy, striped, high, Tan, sandy, Green, leafy, spotted, tall; **Day 3:** 1. oi, oy, oi, oy; 2–3. Answers will vary. **Day 4:** 1. a fable; 2. Answers will vary. 3. most, One day, far away

Page 22
1. gentle, friendly; big, beautiful; split, upper; thick, wool; 2. oy, oi, oy, oy; 3. (left to right) L, S, S, S, L, L; 4. A fable is a made-up story told to teach a lesson. 5. over the mountains, unevenly, momentarily, to the left, accidentally, sideways

Page 23
Day 1: 1. a deep bed of light, loose sand that is full of water; 2. quicksand; 3. (circled) plastic bag, feather, cotton ball; **Day 2:** 1. (circled) honesty, (underlined) teacher, child; 2. (circled) patriotism, (underlined) Americans, country; 3. (circled) love, (underlined) family; 4. (circled) compassion, (underlined) child; **Day 3:** 1. glasses; 2. rolled around; 3. weaken; **Day 4:** 1. homeless; 2. tangled; 3. He is lost. 4. He has another home to visit. There is food there.

Page 24
1. Sand is packed firmly and quicksand is loose and full of water. 2. a ship that has wrecked; something that shields from the wind; a boat with a motor; falling water; 3. (left to right) A, C, A, A, C, A; 4. Answers will vary but may include flu and medicine. 5. with no cares, without a home

Page 25
Day 1: 1. waxing phase; 2. waxing, waning; 3. full moon; **Day 2:** 1. It took Samia only two days to read the book How to Be My Best Friend. 2. Gabe and Peter are watching Toy Store Galore for the third time! 3. The song "Come Ride with Me" is from my favorite movie. **Day 3:** 1. ge, dge, dge, ge; 2. (circled) judge, ledge, message; **Day 4:** 1. Big Bad Wolf; 2. Answers will vary but may include that he was tired from climbing the sand dune. 3. Answers will vary.

Page 26
1. waxing/waning, more/less; 2. "A Light in the Basement," Star City, "Pop the Cop Goes to Town"; 3. ge, ge, dge, dge; 4–5. Answers will vary.

Page 27
Day 1: 1. 570 feet deep and nearly a mile wide; 2. 50,000, million-ton, 570; 3. A; **Day 2:** 1. windier; 2. loudest; 3. taller; 4. closest; **Day 3:** 1. hard work; 2. curious; 3. usual; **Day 4:** 1. to make sure bluebirds could get in but house sparrows and starlings could not; 2. bluebirds, house sparrows, starlings; 3. could not, couldn't

Page 28
1. Answers will vary. 2. (left to right) 2, 2, 3, 3, 2, 3; 3. Answers will vary. 4. (circled) solve crimes, some, rain or snow; 5. would not, she is, where is, has not, could have, you will

Page 29
Day 1: 1. B; 2. unidentified flying object; **Day 2:** 1. use; 2. are; 3. dig; 4. carries; **Day 3:** 1. scr; 2. st; 3. spr; 4. cl; **Day 4:** 1. doll; 2. (underlined) Felicia has a china head, she is over 200 years old, and she has an owner. 2. careless; 3. forgetful

CD-104979 • © Carson-Dellosa

Answer Key

Page 30
1. F, O, F, O; 2. Answers will vary but may include people/sing, corn/grows, kangaroos/hop, skateboards/glide, babies/cry. 3. Check students' work. 4. Answers will vary.

Page 31
Day 1: 1. a type of fungus; 2. common, moist or damp; Answers will vary. **Day 2:** 1. or; 2. because; 3. if; 4. but; **Day 3:** 1. rk; 2. rk; 3. nk; 4. st; **Day 4:** 1. The bat took sides only with the winners. 2. The bat was wishy-washy and not a true friend. 3. Answers will vary.

Page 32
1. probably, type, develop; 2. Jack wants to take violin lessons because his sister has been taking them for years. Nora plays piano by ear since she can't read notes at all. 3. Check students' work. 4. personal traits or qualities; 5. Answers will vary.

Page 33
Day 1: 1. the differences between white and brown pelicans' eating habits; 2. scared; 3. Answers will vary but may include alone/together, down/up, above/below; **Day 2:** 1. Mr. Al Rizzo, 536 Foreman Road, Tucson, Arizona 85712; 2. Mother and I went to the Atlantic Ocean for a day. **Day 3:** 1. pl; 2. st; 3. dr; 4. sw; **Day 4:** 1. Thunder, rain, and heat make seeds grow. 2. thunder; 3. Answers will vary.

Page 34
1. Check students' work. 2. Tommy Carter, 136 Allentown Road, Telford, Pennsylvania 18969; There are more stars in the Milky Way galaxy than we can see. 3. Check students' work. 4. Answers will vary.

Page 35
Day 1: The family in Laura Ingalls Wilder's books faced many hardships. 2. Answers will vary but could include from her own family. 3. Wisconsin, Kansas, Minnesota, South Dakota; **Day 2:** 1. Ms. Teresa Small, 65 Moose Lane, Homer, Alaska 99603; 2. The Smithsonian Museum is in Washington, DC and it is free;

Day 3: 1. ar, ar, ar, er, or, or, ir; **Day 4:** 1. Answers will vary. 2. rain/lane, heat/street; 3. The author thinks rain is beautiful.

Page 36
1. log cabin, Answers will vary. 2. Danny can play "Three Blind Mice" on his flute. The president lives in the White House on 1600 Pennsylvania Avenue. 3. farm/firm/form, barn/born/burn, card, cord, curd; 4. Answers will vary.

Page 37
Day 1: 1. big trees; 2. how redwoods grow to be so tall; 3. to live; **Day 2:** 1. washes, help, scrub, polish; 2. Answers will vary. **Day 3:** 1. g**nome**; 2. crum**b**s; 3. dou**b**t; 4. **w**rist; **Day 4:** 1. B; 2. Answers will vary but may include a search on the internet.

Page 38
1. Answers will vary. 2. Answers will vary but may include team/cheers, school/closes, herd/gallops, Ms. Gupta/laughs, kittens/play. 3. thum**b**, **w**reath, cas**t**le, **k**not; 4. **k**nock, sc**h**oolhouse, **w**rite; Answers will vary.

Page 39
Day 1: 1. Kip Wagner has found sunken treasure. 2–3. Answers will vary. **Day 2:** Bobcats and bears live in the mountains of Virginia. 2. The deer and coyote drink from the stream. 3. The airplane startled the rabbit and the owl. **Day 3:** 1. Answers will vary but may include yell, mad, raise. 2. Answers will vary but may include whisper, calm, drop. **Day 4:** 1. excited; 2. types; 3. outdoors, probably a forest

Page 40
1. Answers will vary. 2. (circled) close/shut, correct/right; 3. add/subtract, easy/difficult; 4. Answers will vary but may include that Danny was not excited about his hiking trip.

Answer Key

Page 41
Day 1: 1. C; 2. a kind of picture writing; 3. to communicate with others; **Day 2:** 1. or; 2. but; 3. so/and; 4. so/and; **Day 3:** 1. A; 2. B;
Day 4: 1. (underlined) surf is pounding and fills his ears, saltwater spray tickles his face, licks his lips, they taste salty, air feels crisp and cool, waves break over his toes; 2. to split the surface; 3. to crack apart

Page 42
1. an ancient kind of picture writing used by Egyptians, 4; 2. (circled) but, nor, and, so; 3. Answers will vary. 4. up to date, Answers will vary. 5. Answers will vary.

Page 43
Day 1: 1. (T in front of) Flu shots are available for people who want them and The flu changes each year, so getting a flu shot every year is good.
Day 2: 1. if; 2. because; 3. unless; 4. Since;
Day 3: 1. unhappy; 2. stopped working; 3. Answers will vary but may include because he is a white dog with black spots. **Day 4:** 1. C; 2. driveway

Page 44
1. A; 2. (circled) unless, if, because, Since; 3. (underlined) un/not afraid, un/not certain, un/cannot be stopped, un/open the latch, It means not or cannot. 4. eye/balls, back/stage, under/dog, mean/while, rain/check, no/where; 5. Answers will vary.

Page 45
Day 1: (circled) nothing tastes as good on pancakes or waffles as maple syrup;
2. (underlined) Maple syrup comes from the sap of maple trees. Just before spring comes, the trees send sugar and water up from their roots to their branches. 3. the sap of maple trees;
Day 2: 1. nor; 2. if; 3. for; 4. since; **Day 3:** (circled) cousin, friend, delight, Then, all; **Day 4:** 1. fiction, A turtle is telling the story. 2. something that hunts other animals for food; 3. prey; 4. Yes, because humans hunt them for their shells.

Page 46
1. O, F, F, O; 2. Answers will vary but could include naughty, rapid, gradually, beautiful. 3. (circled) but/C, if/S, or/C; 4. today, out, should/once; 5. Fiction is a story that is not true. Nonfiction is true and contains facts.

Page 47
Day 1: 1. to inform; 2. hot and wet; 3. Answers will vary. **Day 2:** 1. C, 2. S; 3. CX; 4. the tree's apples; 5. the ocean's waves; 6. the airplanes' pilots; **Day 3:** 1. believe; 2. once; 3. license; 4. mountain; 5. knock; **Day 4:** 1. evening; 2. on the beach; 3. Gabe, Holly

Page 48
1. Answers will vary. 2. B; 3. Answers will vary. 4. suposed/supposed, fourty/forty, minites/minutes; 5. Answers will vary.

Page 49
Day 1: 1. about how Jane Goodall worked with a group of chimps; 2. African jungle; 3. Answers will vary. **Day 2:** What do you do when you need to earn extra money? Nell and I set up a lemonade stand. We made colorful signs to hang around the neighborhood. Dad helped us make cookies and chocolate pretzels. They were really delicious. Can you guess how much money we made? We made over $20! That was a great job!
Day 3: 1–4. Answers will vary. **Day 4:** 1. library; 2. a thing to do; 3. weekend, anything, beanbag, bookworm

Page 50
1. Answers will vary. 2. period, question mark, exclamation mark; 3–4. Answers will vary. 5. Answers will vary but may include eyeball, baseball, sweetheart, fireworks.

CD-104979 • © Carson-Dellosa

Answer Key

Page 51
Day 1: 1. B; 2. (underlined) Long ago, Roman rulers enjoyed eating mountain snow. 3. cream;
Day 2: 1. herself; 2. ourselves; 3. myself; 4. herself; 5. himself; 6. themselves; **Day 3:** 1–4. Answers will vary. **Day 4:** 1. all of the things that surround us; 2. Insects are eating holes in the leaves of his garden plants. 3. We should not use pesticides.

Page 52
1. Romans ate mountain snow. Europeans ate flavored ice. Cream was mixed with ice to make ice cream. 2. himself, myself; 3. Answers will vary. 4. (circled) After the chain on the bicycle broke, (underlined) the wheels would not turn. (circled) when the screen went blank, (underlined) We knew the computer had stopped working.

Page 53
Day 1: 1. because her brothers and sisters were skaters; 2. trained, Answers will vary.
Day 2: 1. run; 2. shouted; 3. frightened; 4. furious;
Day 3: 1. winner, one who excels, Answers will vary. 2. champion (noun), one who excels; champion (verb) to stand up for a cause;
Day 4: 1. a legend; People have passed along the story of a sleeping bear to explain the shape of the Sleeping Bear Dunes. 2. a fictional story that has been passed along to explain something that is real; 3. Answers will vary.

Page 54
1. Answers will vary but may include that she practiced a lot and started young. 2. (left to right) first, tiny, best, female; 3. rinse/clean/scrub, nibble/eat/gobble, big/large/enormous; 4. Answers will vary. 5. Grand Canyon has a very deep canyon. Crater Lake is a lake inside a crater.

Page 55
Day 1: 1. The North Star is easy to find. 2. Because the North Star has helped sailors find their way. 3. C; **Day 2:** 1. bought; 2. sold; 3. brought; 4. said;

Page 56
1. Because Polaris is always in the same spot (but not everywhere). 2. think/thought, meet/met, say/said, fly/flew, leave/left, buy/bought, bring/brought, fight/fought, feed/fed, light/lit; 3. Answers will vary. 4. A dog, Because he is shaggy and barked at a rabbit. 5. fall, spring

Page 57
Day 1: 1. Animal behavior can be a real mystery. 2. a wild rush in many directions; 3. Answers will vary. **Day 2:** 1. House's; 2. nation's; 3. world's; 4. Bush's; **Day 3:** 1. here, hear, there, they're, their; **Day 4:** 1. She had lost her phone. 2. Answers will vary but may include mudroom, backpack, Daylight; 3. Answers will vary.

Page 58
1. Answers will vary but may include narrow, walked, quiet, lost. 2. Ronald Reagan's hometown was Tampico, Illinois. Benjamin Harrison's nickname was "Little Ben." 3. hour, here, knew; 4–5. Answers will vary.

Page 59
Day 1: 1. Answers will vary but may include because it scares people and lives in the snow. 2. Mount Everest; 3. Answers will vary.
Day 2: 1. the girls' bedroom; 2. the monkeys' food; 3. the teachers' decisions; 4. bears' coats, 5. trees' fruit, 6. cows' milk, 7. squirrels' nuts;
Day 3: Answers will vary. **Day 4:** 1. stanza; 2. pillows; 3. children

Page 60
1. Answers will vary. 2. polar bears' thick white fur, bear cubs' mother, seals' flippers; 3–5. Answers will vary.

Page 3:
Day 3: 1. a wild animal (noun) or endure (verb); 2. to be able (verb) or a tin for holding food (noun); 3. covering on a plant (noun) or to yelp (verb); 4. a flower (noun) or to have gotten up (verb); **Day 4:** 1. Sally, Norman; 2. fall, because the leaves are brown and geese are migrating; 3. slow

Answer Key

Page 61
Day 1: 1. Answers will vary. 2. to be separated into groups; 3. (underlined) But, he soon made Rookie of the Year! **Day 2:** 1. The painting is called *Still Life: Vase with Fifteen Sunflowers*. 2. It was painted in August 1888 by Vincent Van Gogh. 3. Van Gogh was living in Arles, France, then. 4. Arles, France, is in Europe. **Day 3:** 1. precipitation/weather conditions such as snow, sleet, rain; 2. archeology/a science in which found objects tell about earlier people; 3. adaptation/the way an animal survives in its environment; 4. global/ having to do with the entire world; **Day 4:** 1. a frozen lake; 2. He likes to fish with him. 3. Nathan thought he had a fish, but it was an old boot.

Page 62
1. Answers will vary. 2. *The Starry Night, The Potato Eaters*; 3. Science: species, ecosystem, recycle; Social Studies: explorer, civilization, America; 4. kitchen, beach; 5. Dan got an idea. Watch the baby.

Page 63
Day 1: 1. a huge mass of slowly moving ice; 2. The glaciers started to melt. 3. rain and melting glacier water filling the holes; **Day 2:** 1. accept; 2. flipper; 3. happy; 4. puddles; 5. addition; 6. alligator; **Day 3:** Answers will vary but may include: 1. stepped/stopped; 2. eat/smell; 3. bat/glove; 4. homework/sandwich; **Day 4:** 1. It is a letter. 2. She has moved away. 3. snake, (underlined) curls into a ball, flips his tail, slithers

Page 64
1–3. Answers will vary. 4. Answers will vary but may include under/over, rain/wind; 5. Answers will vary.

Page 65
Day 1: 1. cocoa beans and bitter spices; 2. Sugar was added. 3. to make the bitter drink sweet; **Day 2:** 1. carried; 2. cried; 3. tried; 4. relied; **Day 3:** 1. (circled) The number of chimpanzees/ in the wild/had been dropping off/for decades. 2. The habits of chimpanzees/who live in the wild/ were studied by Jane Goodall.

3. Jane Goodall learned many things/in the years/ she spent with the chimpanzees. **Day 4:** 1. Hickory is a hamster or gerbil. soft fur, pink ears, runs on a wheel; 2. B; 3. date, greeting, closing, signature

Page 66
1. Answers will vary. 2. tried, carried, married, dried, hurried, copied; 3. (circled) I wish/I could bring home a puppy/from the shelter. Mom rushed/off to her job this morning/without any breakfast. 4. Answers will vary. 5. skunk, frog

Page 67
Day 1: 1. to make large amounts at one time; 2. Answers will vary but may include that it was too expensive. 3. Answers will vary. **Day 2:** iguana, dinosaur, raccoon; **Day 3:** 1–5. Answers will vary. **Day 4:** 1. dogs, (underlined) excited barking, continued to bark, heard a yelp, two hairy animals; 2. bad smell, stink or smell; 3. someone/ thing who is with another, friend or buddy

Page 68
1. Answers will vary. 2. Answers will vary but may include brave, dry, worst, poor. 3. flashlight, magnet, trophy; 4. especially, community, whether; 5. whale, kangaroo, squirrel

Page 69
Day 1: 1. h; 2. willow bark, garlic cloves; 3. B; **Day 2:** Answers will vary but may include: 1. being of help to others; 2. showing interest and kindness; 3. taking care; 4. feeling good and fortunate; 5. without fear; 6. tending to talk a lot; 7. fast; **Day 3:** 1–4. Answers will vary. **Day 4:** 1. at an ocean beach, (underlined) starfish washes up, sand dollar, seashells; 2. Answers will vary but may include to keep them from breaking. 3. starfish, seashells

Page 70
1. k, g, w, b; 2. Answers will vary but may include is full of good spirits, is full of strength, keeps things in order. 3–4. Answers will vary. 5. Answers will vary but may include half, sad, answer, forget.

CD-104979 • © Carson-Dellosa

Answer Key

Page 71

Day 1: 1. returning boomerangs; 2. They could hit a target harder than a stick or stone. **Day 2:** 1. heat before; 2. to not be comfortable; 3. without pain; 4. to not like; 5. middle of the field; 6. to be aware.;7. to be in a state of wonder; 8. having no point; **Day 3:** 1. because; 2. Wednesday; 3. friendly; 4. please; 5. excuse; **Day 4:** 1. fiction; 2. (underlined) One plump squirrel . . . lunch?"; 3. to move quickly

Page 72

1. It spins out and comes back. 2. cen/ti/pede, but/ter/fly, grand/moth/er, mis/un/der/stand; 3. untied, misbehaves, dislikes; 4. ~~favrite~~/favorite, ~~craem~~/cream, ~~ever~~/every, ~~desert~~/dessert, ~~perents~~/parents; 5. Answers will vary.

Page 73

Day 1: 1. correct, wavy or curved, carnival; 2. B; **Day 2:** 1. taller; 2. tallest; 3. more beautifully; 4. more slowly; **Day 3:** 1. no, Answers will vary. 2. no, Answers will vary. **Day 4:** 1. A; 2. an alien; 3. Answers will vary.

Page 74

1–2. Answers will vary. 3. (underlined) alarm rang quietly, jumped off the floor, midnight and already late for dinner, ran over the sidewalk, get there late; 4. fiction, (underlined) warned the alien, Jogi said; 5. Answers will vary.

Page 75

Day 1: 1. full of venom; 2. (underlined) Animals in the desert are different . . . regions. Gila monsters are mostly underground and can go months between meals. Javelinas are able to eat cactus plants with sharp spines. **Day 2:** 1–3. Answers will vary. Check that reasons match choices. **Day 3:** 1. unhappy, happiness, happier; 2. disagree, agreement, agreeable; 3. prepay, payer, payment; 4. preheat, heating, heater; **Day 4:** 1. Yes, Goldilocks and the Three Bears; 2. Answers will vary.

Page 76

1. Answers will vary. 2. Answers will vary but may include hop/jump/leap, pretty/beautiful/gorgeous, funny/amusing/hilarious. 3. dislike/not like, likeable/able to be liked, likely/probably; 4. begs/P, wanted/PT, can play/P; 5. (left to right) 2, 1, 2, 3, 3, 2, 2, 1

Page 77

Day 1: 1. how wolves communicate; 2. communicate; 3. their voices and their bodies; **Day 2:** 1. (underlined) piece of cake, means easy; 2. (underlined) on its last legs, means falling apart; 3. (underlined) give me a hand, means help me; **Day 3:** 1. lotion; 2. tension; 3. caution; 4. permission; 5. mansion; 6. fraction; 7. discussion; 8. pollution; **Day 4:** 1. a mutt; 2. No, because she chases him away when she sees him. 3. Yes, because he has an old identification tag.

Page 78

1. Answers will vary. 2. Answers will vary but may include communicate, speak, chat, mutter, say. 3. She's a potato on a couch./She sits a lot. He was one, big ear./He listened to everything around him. 4. station, adoption, plantation, exhaustion; 5. Answers will vary.

Page 79

Day 1: 1. helping people digest certain foods; 2. helpful, harmful; 3. Bacteria can do many things. **Day 2:** 1–3. Answers will vary but should originate from a thesaurus. 4–5. Answers will vary but should originate from a dictionary. **Day 3:** 1. nice, cereal, recess; 2. cable, candle, castle; 3. circus; **Day 4:** 1. It is on the threatened species list. 2. (underlined) It's tough being a turtle. Some humans make our lives difficult. But, not all is doom and gloom. I think they'll win! (circled) I'm on the threatened species list. They hunt us for our shells! They use them to make jewelry. Some people eat turtle meat and eggs. People also drive across turtle paths. And, there are so many of them on our beaches. Other people are working to save us. 3. difficult, jewelry

Answer Key

Page 80

1. Bacteria are among the smallest forms of life. Diseases are caused by bacteria. 2. Answers will vary but should originate from a thesaurus. 3. S, K, K, S, K, S; 4. Answers will vary. 5. (circled) understand, holiday, envelope, evergreen

Page 81

Day 1: 1. how fingernails and toenails grow; 2. base to tip; 3. cells of hard skin; **Day 2:** 3, 5, 2, 4, 1; **Day 3:** 1. hu/man, O, C; 2. hap/py, C, O; 3. si/lent, O, C; 4. den/tist, C, C; apron, C, C; **Day 4:** 1. A; 2. midday; 3. prairie

Page 82

1. Answers will vary. 2. Answers will vary but may include sandbox, everyone, woodwind, upstairs, boathouse. 3. 2, 1, 4, 3; 4. sad/der, C, C; ho/tel, O, C; pre/tend, O, C; nap/kin, C, C

Page 83

Day 1: 1. a puzzle that needs to be solved; 2. An unusual animal mystery involves birds and ants. 3. seen, observed; **Day 2:** (underlined) rarely, today, tomorrow, Then, finally, Afterward, Finally, Immediately; **Day 3:** 1. Answers will vary but may include photograph, telegraph, autograph. 2. Answers will vary but may include telescope, periscope, microscope. 3. Answers will vary but may include telephone, microphone, phonics. **Day 4:** 1. rollercoaster; 2. first person; 3. I was afraid.

Page 84

1. Answers will vary. 2. Answers will vary but may include baby, yell, talk, wrong, scared, love. 3. First, So, Then, Finally; 4. Answers will vary but may include reporter, aquarium, geometry.

Page 85

Day 1: 1. types of weather; 2. hail, rain, sleet, snow, mist; 3. scorching; 4. freezing; **Day 2:** 1. yellow; 2. correctly; 3. week; 4. enjoy; **Day 3:** 1. engine, giant; 2. goal, game; 3. garage, baggage; **Day 4:** 1. a waterfall; 2. gave; 3. village; 4. He gave each animal a special power.

Page 86

1. Answers will vary. 2. (circled) cold, sink, minute, smile; 3. G, J, J, J, G, J; 4–5. Answers will vary.

Page 87

Day 1: 1. They were each African American. 2. Matthew Henson; 3. Shirley Chisholm; **Day 2:** 1. (circled) not, no; 2. (circled) never, nobody; 3. (circled) None, weren't; Check students' work. **Day 3:** 1. movement of air; 2. to turn in a circle; 3. to bend forward at the waist; 4. loops tied together to top a gift; **Day 4:** 1. to write about carnivorous plants; 2. meat-eating

Page 88

1. Answers will vary. 2. (circled) ever, anything, ever, was; 3. dry land with few plants, to abandon; a line of items or objects that runs horizontally, to move a boat along; 4. Answers will vary.

CD-104979 • © Carson-Dellosa